IMITATING
CHRIST

R. T.
KENDALL

Charisma
HOUSE
A STRANG COMPANY

Most Strang Communications/Charisma House/Siloam/FrontLine/Realms products are available at special quantity discounts for bulk purchase for sales promotions, premiums, fund-raising, and educational needs. For details, write Strang Communications/Charisma House/Siloam/FrontLine/Realms, 600 Rinehart Road, Lake Mary, Florida 32746, or telephone (407) 333-0600.

Imitating Christ by R. T. Kendall
Published by Charisma House
A Strang Company
600 Rinehart Road
Lake Mary, Florida 32746
www.charismahouse.com

Unless otherwise noted, all Scripture quotations are from Holy Bible, New International Version. Copyright © 1973, 1978, 1984, International Bible Society. Used by permission.

Scripture quotations marked KJV are from the King James Version of the Bible.

Scripture quotations marked NAS are from the New American Standard Bible. Copyright © 1960, 1962, 1963, 1968, 1971, 1972, 1973, 1975, 1977 by the Lockman Foundation. Used by permission. (www.Lockman.org)

Scripture quotations marked NKJV are from the New King James Version of the Bible. Copyright © 1979, 1980, 1982 by Thomas Nelson, Inc., publishers. Used by permission.

Cover design by John Hamilton Design
www.johnhamiltondesign.com

Library of Congress Cataloging-in-Publication Data:

Kendall, R. T.
   Imitating Christ / R.T. Kendall.
      p. cm.
   ISBN-13: 978-1-59979-055-8 (trade paper) 1. Jesus Christ--Example. 2. Christian life.
I. Title.
   BT304.2.K46 2007
   248.4--dc22

                              2006030247

This book was previously published in Great Britain as *Meekness and Majesty* by Christian Focus Publications, ISBN 1-871-676-878, copyright © 1992, 2000.

07 08 09 10 11 — 987654321
Printed in the United States of America

TO RANDY AND NANCY

Contents

Meekness and majesty, manhood and deity,
In perfect harmony, the Man who is God:
Lord of eternity dwells in humanity,
Kneels in humility and washes our feet.

Father's pure radiance, perfect in innocence,
Yet learns obedience to death on a cross:
Suffering to give us life,
Conquering through sacrifice;
And as they crucify, prays, "Father, forgive."

Wisdom unsearchable, God the invisible,
Love indestructible in frailty appears.
Lord of infinity, stooping so tenderly,
Lifts our humanity to the heights of His throne.

O what a mystery, meekness and majesty:
Bow down and worship, for this is your God,
This is your God!*

—Graham Kendrick

Foreword

When I was asked whether I minded if R. T. Kendall used the title of my hymn "Meekness and Majesty" for the UK version of this book, I had no hesitation in agreeing, considering it an honor to be associated in such a way. However, when I heard the book would be published in the United States, I felt doubly honored and delighted to know that he had employed some of the lyrics as chapter titles. If I had only one complaint, it is that I feel he has been overgenerous in associating my poor efforts with the masterpieces of my hymn-writing hero Charles Wesley!

As someone who has had no formal theological training and who depends upon the critique given by qualified friends to save me from the contemporary equivalent of being burnt at the stake as a heretic, I approach such themes in fear and trembling. In the case of the aforementioned hymn, it was a conversation with Clive Calver that saved me from certain immolation when he saw that the original draft for the line "dwells in humanity" read "clothed in humanity." Poetically satisfying perhaps, but unfortunately reminiscent of an ancient heresy that claimed that the Son of God was clothed with humanity only on a temporary basis.

If any credit is being dispensed, I must be swift to mention the name of the late American preacher and author A. W. Tozer, in whose writings I first saw the words *meekness* and *majesty* side by side. It was after the hymn had been completed that on re-reading the chapter I saw in his inspiring treatise on the subject a plea that some day someone would write a hymn on the meekness and majesty of Christ. Perhaps it was his prayers that set it all in motion, and the momentum will be increased as more songwriters and authors mine this inexhaustible seam.

I have a dear friend whose love for Jesus shines unusually brightly and whose spiritual hearing is unusually clear. Some time ago he asked the Lord to tell him where the powers of darkness would concentrate their assault upon the church most fiercely in the period in which we are now living. The answer he received was "against the uniqueness of My Son, and the value of a human soul." In a climate of growing pluralism, syncretism, deception, heresy, and confusion, we need the church to arise and become imitators of Christ to the world. That is why I heartily welcome this book, *Imitating Christ.* I am confident that those readers who desire to be true worshipers, those who worship the Father in spirit and truth, will find here a treasure chest of truth that will intoxicate their spirits to worship.

—Graham Kendrick

Preface

When I wrote the UK version of this book, the managing editor of Christian Focus Inc., Malcolm Maclean, had kindly approached me about writing a book based on Philippians 2:5–11. Since I had preached on this passage in 1986, I felt there might be something in his call. The sermons were subsequently typed from a tape recorder, edited with a view to making them readable, then presented to me for approval. What follows, then, is a severely edited report of my preaching on this most sublime section of the New Testament.

We considered several titles for the UK version—from *Christ Vindicated* to *Let God Clear Your Name*, but I had no peace that we had gotten it right. I turned to my friend Lyndon Bowring, who often comes up with ingenious sermon titles for me. But he too was at sea this time! He turned to his wife, Celia, who in seconds said, "I've got it—*Meekness and Majesty*."

There was only one thing to do: go to Graham Kendrick on bended knee and ask for his permission! I can say that not only did he not hesitate, but he also graciously provided a commendation. I have regarded "Meekness and Majesty" as Graham's greatest hymn (so far), and the thought of having this magnificent work associated with my own book was almost overwhelming. What is more, some phrases from his song provided chapter titles so naturally that I am tempted to say he wrote it for me!

I have been saying for years—I'd like to think I was the first—that Graham Kendrick is a modern-day Charles Wesley. Singing "Restore, O Lord, the Honor of Your Name" almost brings me to tears every time. The same is true of "Shine, Jesus, Shine." I could go on and on. But surely he will never excel "Meekness and Majesty"! I love that title.

When my American publisher suggested changing the title to *Imitating Christ*, at first it was jarring, but then I came to the understanding that my American audience would more clearly identify the new title with the concept of becoming more like Christ.

I believe I have written a book that should serve to unite Christians of various denominational and theological persuasions more than any book I have published so far. For surely we all have this in common: the desire to be more like Jesus. This is what this book is all about.

I pray for the reader's indulgence when he or she comes across two things that could be disconcerting. First, my love for alliteration (words beginning with the same letter), a sermonic device that is almost second nature to me. Secondly, the switching back and forth between the New International Version and the King James Version of the Bible. We had not moved to the NIV when I preached the sermons, but herein we have changed most of the references to the NIV.

However, the scholar in me prefers "mind of Christ" as the translation of Philippians 2:5, as also "form of God" in verse 6. And yet the NIV translation is perfectly good, and this most certainly is true with verse 9: "*the* name that is above every name," a vital grammatical point the KJV sadly misses.

What haunts me most, though, as I present this book to the reader is my own failure to come up to the standard of humility and Christlikeness the text calls for. But God isn't finished with me yet!

I want to thank Lillian McAnally and Deborah Moss for the devoted work they have done in further editing this book. I express appreciation to Barbara Dycus for her advice and, most of all, to Stephen Strang for graciously opening a door for publishing my books in the United States.

I dedicate this book fondly to one of our favorite couples in the world: Mr. and Mrs. Randy Wall of Key Largo, Florida.

—R. T. KENDALL
www.rtkendallministries.com

Philippians 2:5–11

Your attitude should be the same as that of Christ Jesus:

Who, being in very nature God,
did not consider equality with God something to be
grasped,
but made himself nothing,
taking the very nature of a servant,
being made in human likeness.
And being found in appearance as a man,
he humbled himself
and became obedient to death—even death on a cross!
Therefore God exalted him to the highest place
and gave him the name that is above every name,
that at the name of Jesus every knee should bow,
in heaven and on earth and under the earth,
and every tongue confess that Jesus Christ is Lord,
to the glory of God the Father.

Chapter 1

MEEKNESS

Your attitude should be the same as that of Christ Jesus.

—Philippians 2:5

Most believers genuinely desire to imitate Christ. Obviously you do, or you would not have picked up this book! You want to exemplify a Christlike attitude in all you say and do, but often you fall short of the goal. And then you beat yourself down when you do fall short, but that is not what He wants you to do. The apostle Paul in a letter to the Corinthian church said, "Imitate me, just as I also imitate Christ" (1 Cor. 11:1, NKJV).

We are not entirely sure how the apostle Paul planned his letters when he wrote them. We do know that some were written to answer questions. For instance, the letters to Thessalonica deal largely with answering questions that the Christians there had asked about the Second Coming of Christ. Similarly, in his letters to the Corinthians, Paul answers one question after another. When he wrote to the Galatians, he had to deal with the specific problem of the Judaizers. We know that much about the way he wrote: he often responded to actual questions or areas of difficulty of which he was aware.

The question, then, is did he know all that he was going to say, or did he think of it as he moved along? It is interesting to ponder whether he always knew what he was going to write. Did Paul not rather compose sometimes as he went along, inspired by what immediately preceded? With regard to this section from the Book of Philippians that we are about to consider, I could not help but wonder.

Did Paul Compose This Section?

These verses, Philippians 2:5–11, comprise one of the most magnificent sections in the New Testament. So arresting and full are these verses that I am bound to ask, did Paul plan this section from the beginning of the epistle, or was it a sudden burst from the heart when he exclaimed, "Ah, your attitude should be the same...," stirred up by what he wrote in the first four verses.

It is widely accepted that verses 6–11 were an early Christian confession in poetic form. Some translations, you will notice, translate these verses like a poem. It is thought, therefore, that Paul incorporated it into his letter. Some think it was a hymn that was part of the liturgy of the church in Palestine, that it was originally written in Aramaic and sung as a hymn there. In other words, some scholars believe that verses 6–11 were not really written by Paul at all, but that he simply included this hymn in the letter. There is no way to know for sure. In heaven, we can ask Paul. It probably will not be the first question we will want to ask him, but we can ask him then.

Some scholars are of the opinion that 1 Corinthians 13, known as "the love chapter," was also a kind of liturgical hymn in the church. A friend of mine completed a PhD in Cambridge on 1 Corinthians

12–14. His conclusion was that 1 Corinthians 13 was, in fact, Paul's own words and that he wrote it. And that is what I think is true about Philippians 2:5–11. I do not believe that he merely incorporated it. If he had chosen to do so, there is nothing wrong with that. But I suspect that Palestinian Christianity, from what we know about it, was too simple, if I may put it that way, to have come up with such a depth of theological thought as is found in these verses.

The passage begins with Paul's appeal to the example that Christ set for the church. Because of this he calls the church to humility, the means by which it will obtain greatness (these are words used interchangeably by Paul). It is also in following the example of Christ that the church will suffer for its belief. Nevertheless, he uses the example of Christ to show how to handle this suffering. In all he pleads for unity in the church before beginning this passage, verses 5–11, which explores the example that Jesus set for us and to which he appeals.

Yet Paul does not use the word *example*. He might have done so, just as Peter did in 1 Peter 2:21 where he refers to Christ leaving us an example. But Paul did not say, "Let this example be your example." Rather he said, "Your attitude should be the same as that of Christ Jesus," or as the King James Version translates it, which I will use when quoting this verse, "Let this mind be in you, which was also in Christ Jesus."

He said in verse 3, "Do nothing out of selfish ambition or vain conceit, but in *humility* [lowliness of *mind*, KJV] consider others better than yourselves" (emphasis added). So in verse 5 he says, "Let this *mind* be in you." Some scholars believe that verse 5 should be translated, "Let this mind be among you," as if appealing that there might be a collective consensus with the mind of Christ. Well, there is certainly nothing wrong in wanting that, but that is not what Paul says. Clearly, he writes, "Let this mind be *in you*, which was also in Christ Jesus" (emphasis added). He wants the Philippians to subjectively experience something, namely, the mind of Christ, on an individual level.

What does he mean, therefore, by the mind of Christ? Well, it can be seen in two ways: objectively and subjectively. Objectively, Paul tells us that the mind of Christ was, "Who, being in very nature God, did not consider equality with God something to be grasped, but made himself nothing, taking the very nature of a servant, being made in human likeness. And being found in appearance as a man, he humbled himself and became obedient to death—even death on a cross" (vv. 6–8). Objectively, that is what caused the events of Christ's Incarnation to happen.

Subjectively, that mind of Christ is to be ours in experience. In short, it is to give up what we thought was rightfully ours. Thus, when Paul says, "Let this *mind* be in you," he does not mean, "Let the IQ that Jesus had be in you." He does not mean His intellect or His learning. Then what does Paul mean? We need to get closer to understanding this phrase "the mind of Christ."

Our #1 A.I.M.

If we are to have a better understanding of the phrase "the mind of Christ," then it can be understood in relation to three characteristics: attitude, initiative, motivation. The acrostic that heads this section helps to remind us what is entailed.

Attitude

By attitude, I mean perspective. Paul said that Jesus took upon Himself "the very nature of a servant." This is the way Jesus saw

Himself, as a servant, the whole time He lived. But it was not only a self-image; it was a passion with Him. You could call it a preoccupation. It was all He thought about, a certain kind of attitude. In a word: meekness. Quiet obedience, making no protest. It was a lifestyle. It was His pursuit. He followed it through again and again. This brings us to a question: Do we want the mind of Christ to be in us? How much do we want it? For Jesus it was a perspective, a passion, a pursuit. He lived this way.

Now, some may say, "Well, I did that once. I know what that is." But with Jesus it was an ongoing lifestyle, and this is the way that we are called to be from now on.

Perhaps you think that you will try living like this for one week—perhaps to see what it is like. Or you may want to do it for a while, but then you want to take a vacation from it. You say, "I don't have to live this way now; I have paid my dues. I have been living like that. Now I will live another way."

We will never have the mind of Christ in us until this becomes a perspective, which is a passion and a pursuit, a lifestyle with which we are going to live twenty-four hours a day, every day of our lives. No change!

The content of the attitude

To get a little closer to the meaning we must look at what this attitude involves. Essentially, it is a self-emptying attitude. In later chapters we will take a closer look at verse 6, where we read that Jesus relinquished what rightfully belonged to Him. The King James Version captures the self-effacing quality in the next verse: He "made himself of no reputation." What kind of an attitude would we need to make ourselves "of no reputation"? Are we like that? Do we not place more importance on what other people think of us? We are always concerned for our reputation, yet here is one who made Himself of no reputation.

Involved in content of this is the attitude of *self-expendability*: "being found in appearance as a man, he humbled himself and became obedient to death—even death on a cross!" (v. 8). What does this mean? Paul is talking about the fact that Jesus never took Himself seriously. This is an amazing virtue. Most of us know what it is to take ourselves seriously. It is one of the most refreshing things you can ever come across, and it is an exceedingly rare thing, to meet someone who does not take himself seriously.

We might think ourselves so important that we say, "Well, I have to be there," or "I'm needed," or "What will happen if I'm not there?" And then we become too sensitive and easily offended. We walk around wearing our hearts on our sleeves. Anything can—and does—upset us. This is because we do not think of ourselves as being expendable. But Jesus, who was the greatest gift there ever was to the human race, made no such claims. He humbled Himself even to death on a cross. Greatness is having this conviction of self-expendability.

Initiative

The second characteristic is initiative. Three things sum up what I mean by Christlike initiative. First, it is a *conscious* commitment to count the cost. We count the cost, and we know exactly what we are doing. It is not what the existentialists call the "leap of faith," a leap in the dark. That is not Christian thinking. No, we count the cost; we know exactly what is at stake. With Jesus, this was an acknowledgment of a possession: He "did not consider equality with God something to be grasped" (v. 6). Moreover, He was in the form of

God. He knew that He was God, and yet we are told that He did not cling to His deity.

We are told to have the same kind of initiative. We look carefully at what we feel is rightfully ours, and yet we let it go. The difference between Jesus and us is that we merely *think* it is rightfully ours, but with Jesus, it *was* rightfully His. He was in the form *of* God. With us, we only impute to ourselves this right. You may say, "Ah, just a minute; it is mine because God gave it to me." But I answer, Godhood and all the glory that goes with it was intrinsically His, yet He did not see it as something onto which He should hold. *The point is that He let it go.* Therefore, "let this mind be in you." This was the initiative.

Second, as well as being a conscious commitment, it was also one that was *irrevocable*. You see, here is the difficulty with us. As a pastor, this has in many ways been my greatest dilemma: understanding how people claim to be committed, and then within a matter of weeks or months, they are not committed anymore. A commitment is a commitment, yet we do not want to inconvenience ourselves; we can think of every reason to change. Circumstances must never change the commitment. So often with us circumstances cause us to reassess. But with Jesus it was a conscious, irrevocable commitment; He let it go, and He never looked back: "Let this mind be in you."

Third, it is also a *courageous* commitment. Ronald Reagan once said, "The future doesn't belong to the fainthearted; it belongs to the brave."

There are two reasons why taking the initiative in this way requires courage, one of which follows from the other.

First, it is because it is a call to *leadership*. You see, the mind of Christ means initiative, and that means not only is it a voluntary conscious decision, but also that it is taking the lead. You may say, "Well, I am not a natural-born leader," but would Paul put anything on us that is impossible? I promise you that God will never ask you to do what He knows you cannot do. He will never ask you to elevate yourself to the level of your incompetence.

But you see, courage is not a natural endowment. Nobody has courage like this, except by the Holy Spirit, and when Paul says, "Let this mind be in you," he is saying, "If you will take the initiative, grace will be there." So it means taking the lead. Perhaps you wait to see if others do it. Instead, you must do it, because it is between you and God, and God sees you. Many difficulties arise today because of a lack of commitment and a dearth of real *greatness* in the world. Most leaders are followers. Did you know that? What they do is wet a finger and then hold it up in the air to see which way the wind is blowing; then they run out in front and say, "I am leading this group," trying to get the credit. A true leader is one who is not looking over his shoulder to see who is following. If he does look over his shoulder, he might find there is nobody following him.

Second, it requires courage also because this call to leadership involves a call to *loneliness.* Taking the lead is the loneliest position in the world, and you cannot look back and see who is following you. You do not have that luxury. Jesus put it like this:

No one who puts his hand to the plow and looks back is fit for service in the kingdom of God.

—LUKE 9:62

"Let this mind be in you, which was also in Christ Jesus." Imitating Christ's initiative is never an easy task.

Motivation

What do you suppose motivated Jesus? It was *reverence* for His Father. If you want to know something about the mind of Christ, I challenge you to study the Gospel of John and look at the relationship Jesus had with His Father. He put it like this, for example, in John 5:30:

> By myself I can do nothing; I judge only as I hear, and my judgment is just, for I seek not to please myself but him who sent me.

Then later in that chapter He said something, a verse that many years ago gripped me and I hope will grip you:

> How can you believe if you accept praise from one another, yet make no effort to obtain the praise that comes from the only God?

—JOHN 5:44

If that kind of thinking will grip you, then you are a candidate to think about the mind of Christ.

All that a preacher or writer may say or expound upon will only become relevant once there is embedded in you a true fear of God. And that has to happen between you and God. As long as you are hoping that someone else will notice you, and that is how you get your motivation, then your motivation is phony, and it will not last. Perhaps you want your church leaders to notice your endeavors, and this drives you to carry on. But this cannot work. Something, sooner or later, has to happen so that your honor comes from God. That is all that matters. Then you are not looking to see who else notices you: you are consumed with the passion of wanting *God* to notice you, taking your orders from above. A preacher may preach his heart out, but he can only pray that God, somehow, will get through. Then suddenly, you will be aware that it is not his voice you are hearing, but the Spirit giving you no rest.

Jesus' motivation was reverence. It was also *righteousness.* He said in Matthew 5:17: "I have not come to abolish [the law] but to fulfill [it]." Hebrews 10:7 quotes from a psalm, "I have come to do your will, O God." Jesus humbled Himself and actually put Himself under the law. Now we are not under the law. Christ fulfilled it for us, but we are under the law of Christ, which is far grander and loftier (1 Cor. 9:21; Gal. 6:2).

I do not blame those who want to put us back under the law. It is a substandard way to live, and it is an easy way out: you can have hate in your heart and live like that; you can lust and live like that. But put yourself under the law of Christ. You do not need to worry about the externals; you will be moral, you will be clean, you will be godly, but in your heart there will be a mellowness, a brokenness, and a spirit of self-effacement and self-expendability.

May God help us to see it. And that was the motivation of Jesus, who was above the law but went under it for us, fulfilling it for us. Now we are under Him who did it all that we might be saved.

But there is another thing that motivated Him, and this may surprise you. Did you know that Jesus was motivated by *reward*? I hear people say, "Don't talk to me about reward. It is another way of displaying false humility. I don't want reward or recognition. I am just a humble servant of God. I am going to do it because it is right." By saying such things you are trying to upstage Jesus, and I marvel at this. Jesus as a man was motivated by reward.

Let us fix our eyes on Jesus, the author and perfecter of our faith, who for the joy set before him endured the cross, scorning its shame, and sat down at the right hand of the throne of God.

—Hebrews 12:2

He knew there was joy out there, and He was waiting for it. He knew too that He would get it then, not now.

For you see, the reward is not here below. Sometimes God does reward us on earth. He can do it, but if that is your motive, then again it is not right. The reward that motivated Jesus was that which was beyond this life, and He was willing to wait until He went to heaven. Jesus' motivation was waiting for the reward in heaven.

Do we know what kind of reward it will be? Well, I cannot be sure; this matter of reward is a great mystery to me. It certainly meant a lot to Paul. He said, "There is in store for me the crown of righteousness" (2 Tim. 4:8). In 1 Corinthians 9:27, he had some uncertainty whether he would get the prize. He said:

I beat my body and make it my slave so that after I have preached to others, I myself will not be disqualified for the prize.

That was the most abhorrent thought that Paul could imagine: that he himself could be rejected in terms of not getting the reward. Yet just before he died, he said to Timothy, "I have fought the good fight…I have kept the faith" (2 Tim. 4:7).

I do not know whether it is a literal crown that Paul spoke of receiving, but I suspect the grandest moment of all would just be to hear Jesus say, as we find in the parable of the talents in Matthew 25, "Well done." I want to hear, "Well done." I cannot imagine anything greater than that. I will do anything I know to get it.

It is like my friend Sergei Nicolaiev, who was walking with me late one night in Estonia, said, "When I get to heaven, I only want one thing: I want to hear from the lips of Jesus Himself one word—'Good.'"

Jesus endured the cross; He despised the shame because of the joy set before Him. I want that, and that is the motivation contained in this verse, "Let this mind be in you." Do you want to hear Jesus say, "Good"? I can tell you how it will happen: if you "let this mind be in you" and allow your relationship with Him to become harmonious.

Chapter 2

IN PERFECT HARMONY

Who, being in very nature God, did not consider equality with God something to be grasped...

—PHILIPPIANS 2:6

In our quest to become imitators of Christ and become Christlike-minded, we come to what I consider the most sublime section of Philippians, perhaps even the most sublime passage of the whole New Testament. It is Philippians 2:6. It is, however, not a very easy passage, as we will see.

In the context of this section, Paul is simply trying to use Jesus as a supreme example of what it is to give up what is rightfully one's own. In the previous chapter we defined humility as being willing to give up what we feel is rightfully ours. And Jesus is seen here as the example Paul uses in this general call to humility, to suffering, and for the basis of unity in the body of Christ. So Paul says, "Let this mind be in you, which was also in Christ Jesus" (v. 5).

Verse 6 reads, and this is the verse that I will deal with in this chapter, "Who, being in very nature God, did not consider equality with God something to be grasped." Now it would probably be wrong to make too much of the so-called Christological implications of verse 6 and the following verses. (*Christology* is the study of the theological interpretation of the person and work of Christ.) Paul himself would possibly want us to look elsewhere for our foundation of the doctrine of Christ. However, the implications are there, and we shall look at them. What is important to understand is that Paul is not necessarily trying to prove Christ's deity here; he takes it for granted. These Philippians already believe this, so he is not out to prove that Jesus Christ is God; it is precisely because He is God that Paul can speak as he does. And so I refer to this expression as it appears in the King James Version's translation of verse 6, "form of God." What does he mean by *form of God*?

The Form of God

We can see that this is not mainly an attempt to prove Christ's deity. I want us to be theologically sharp, like Paul. Paul was a soulwinner, but he was also theologically minded.

You know, it is an ambition that I have for my readers that we would become theologically minded. As a small boy, I was always interested in theology, and my pastor always used to say that he had never seen a boy quite like me. I just seemed to have a theological mind.

Presently, there is a great dearth of clear, theological thinking. I believe that I have a responsibility to be clear, to be sound, to be understood, to be helpful, to be exactly right. Most people are not going to read the great theological tomes of the past, and what they get in preaching and teaching is going to be all the instruction that most people will get. Once we train ourselves to be theologically sharp, we can be simultaneously soulwinners and theologians. It is never enough to be one without the other. We all know this is true.

We want to understand Paul in this passage.

Now when Paul refers to the phrase "form of God" in verse 6, the word *form* comes from the Greek word *morphe*. It is only used three times in the New Testament—twice in this section—in verse 6, "Who being in the *form* of God" (KJV), and again in verse 7, "he took upon himself the *form* of a servant" (KJV). The other use is in Mark 16:12, referring to Jesus after He was raised from the dead: "afterward Jesus appeared in a different *form* to two of them." (This is obviously a reference to Luke 24 and the two men on the road to Emmaus, where Jesus appeared to them, at least for a while, in another form.)

The question is, why did Paul not simply say "God"? Why did he not say "who being God"? He could have, because he believed that. But had he said that, he would not have been able to use the word that he uses in the next verse, which says that he "made himself of no reputation" (KJV) or "emptied Himself" (NAS). So Paul had to make a choice whether to emphasize what Jesus gave up or to emphasize that He was God. Paul is not questioning that Jesus was God. The point that I am making is that Paul talks about the *form of God* so that he can refer to the fact that Jesus emptied Himself and took upon Himself another form—the form of a servant.

Now, this is important, because there emerged in Sweden in the nineteenth century what became known as Kenotic Christology. It comes from the Greek word, *ekenosen*, which means "He emptied" Himself. The Kenotic theory emerged when some Lutheran Swedish theologians said that God emptied Himself, which meant to some of them that Jesus ceased to be God while He was on earth. That, however, is a heresy and is why Paul did *not* say "who being God," because Jesus could not have emptied Himself of His deity.

The Swedish theologians naturally claimed that this distinction did not exist.

Keep in mind that Paul was not attempting to prove Christ's eternal deity, but rather he was trying to show what Jesus left behind. It was only from the assumption of Christ's deity that Paul could speak at all about Him having the "form of God," for the dominant theme in Paul's mind was Christ's humiliation. The context is governed by verse 4, when Paul said, "Each of you should look not only to your own interests but also to the interests of others." So this word *morphe*, meaning "form," came first in Paul's order of thought because this is the point he wanted to make. This is why he uses the word "form" of God. It refers to Christ in His preincarnate *majesty*.

Jesus was equal with God because He was God. John 1:1 reads, "In the beginning was the Word, and the Word was with God, *and the Word was God*" (emphasis added). What was it He left behind? Not deity. He left something else behind, but He never ceased to be God. He was God from the very moment that He entered the womb of the Virgin Mary in Nazareth, but He did leave something behind. What was it? This is what we will be examining in this and subsequent chapters.

When we read verse 6, we find that the words are not particularly easy to understand. The translation in the King James Version is not helpful. The Greek literally reads, and the NIV brings this out, that Jesus did not consider equality with God something to be held on to or *to be grasped*. So I ask, what is Paul's purpose in writing this? He is reminding his readers that they must relinquish what Christ has relinquished—possession, perception, and position.

Possession

I use the word *possession* because Paul, in saying, "Who being in the form of God" (KJV), uses a Greek word to indicate that Jesus was in full possession of the divine nature. Paul did not use the simple verb "to be"; he used a word that means "to be by nature." Jesus was in the form of God *by nature*. He possessed deity from the beginning. In other words, long before He entered the womb of the Virgin Mary…long before He ever created the angels…long before there was anything, when there was nothing but God, there was also the Word that was with God. Jesus did not *become* the Son of God; He *always was* the Son of God.

When I look at the word *possession*, I think of a question I once heard someone voice: "Can we trust God to keep for us what He has given, never laying hold of it ourselves in our natural desire for possession?" What God gives, He gives. We need not struggle to retain it; indeed, if we grasp it fervently and hold on, we may risk losing it. Only what we have let go in committal to Him becomes, in fact, really ours.

Let me now ask this question. In terms of a possession, what is it that you are trying to hold on to? Jesus possessed by nature the form of God. He was *omniscient*, which means He was all wise; He was *omnipresent*, which means He was everywhere; He was *omnipotent*, which means He was all powerful. But instead He took upon Himself the form of a servant, and all of this was surrendered in measure. As a man, the wisdom He had, He had to learn. We are told that He increased in wisdom and stature. (See Luke 2:52.) He could only be in one place at a time, and His omnipotence, although at His disposal (as when He performed miracles), was accompanied by a perfect faith in God. He came to serve God.

What is it that you are trying to hold on to? Are you willing to be a servant? Could it be that you are trying to hold on to something that God says to let go of? Are you a natural-born manipulator? Maybe you are trying to manipulate your wife? Or your husband? Are you trying to hold on to your home? Are you trying to hold on to your job? Are you trying to hold on to your money? God have mercy on you if you are trying to hold on to *God's* money! Are you trying to hold on to your property? To your fiancé? Are you trying to hold on to your plans for the future? Are you trying to hold on to a gift that God has given you? Could it be that your problem is that you are holding on to yourself?

Paul said in 1 Corinthians 6:19–20: "Do you not know that…you are not your own; you were bought with a price." Could it be that you are taking yourself too seriously? By taking yourself too seriously, you are becoming a nervous wreck. You cannot even have a decent sense of peace with yourself and with others, and you are falling apart. The way that Paul tells us to live is the best way to live; it is the way of peace. Could it be, really, that you are taking yourself too seriously? Are you afraid of what would happen if you were to let go of yourself? Are you afraid of what you would be like if you did let go of yourself? Jesus did not cling to what was His by right: *Let this mind be in you.*

Perception

The Son of God, before He became flesh, perceived what He was; He knew so exactly. It was not merely an opinion He held about Himself or an empty claim He made. He *was* equal with God. He saw it clearly, and there was no room for false humility or modesty here. He knew He was God, equal with the Father and the Holy Spirit both in time and essence. He was God from all eternity, or to put it another way, not one person of the Godhead preceded the other in time. The Father, the Word, and the Spirit coexisted from all eternity. Jesus, in His prayer in John 17, referred to the glory that He had with the Father before the world was.

We can summarize this by asking some questions:

- *Who* is Paul referring to? He says, "Let this mind be in you, which was always in Christ Jesus, who [talking about Jesus Christ], being in the form of God" (Phil. 2:5–6, KJV).

- *When* is he referring to? In eternity before He entered Mary's womb in Nazareth, nine months before His blessed birth in Bethlehem.

- *Where* was He? Paul asks. He was in heaven, in the spiritual realm with God and the angels.

- *What* did He do? We are told that He did not regard equality with God as something to be held on to, but He "emptied Himself" (v. 7, NAS).

- *Why?* Because of the cross: "Being found in appearance as a man, he humbled himself and became obedient to death—even death on a cross" (v. 8).

- *How* did He do it? He entered the womb of a Jewish virgin, in Nazareth. Paul says in Galatians 4:4, "When the time had fully come, God sent his Son, born of a woman, born under law."

Perception relates to our opinion and how we see things. Are you having a running argument with somebody at the moment? Arguing with your spouse? Having a problem at the office? You are just sticking to your guns on something, and everybody but you can see that you are being ridiculous, but you say that you know that you are right. You are making the situation miserable by being a difficult person to work with. Is that possible?

Are you afraid to admit to the possibility that you could be wrong? Are you afraid of what might happen if you lost the argument? Do you worry about what other people would think about you if you gave in or someone just showed that you had gotten it wrong?

Now Jesus had a perception about Himself, that He *was equal with God.* But He did not think it necessary to hold on to that. In becoming like us He was not even omniscient. This may shock you, but He did not know everything. He admitted He did not know the day or the hour of His own coming. He had to learn.

In addition, Jesus *was right.* His opinion was infallibly right, but He even let that go. You say, "Well, I know I've got it right. I can't let it go." Jesus did. The amazing thing is that God Almighty did not even take Himself seriously in this sense. That is your example, and yet you cherish your opinion. Why do you not just be like Jesus? He was right, and He let it go. You could be wrong, and if you are wrong, how much better that you let it go. By the way, if you are right, the truth will come out. It will win in the end. You do not have to do a thing about it. Let Jesus be your example.

"That," you say, "would be surrendering my integrity." That is your pride! Oh, how easy it is to hide behind a principle, when it is just our pride.

Position

Let's examine prestige, our place of security, which we find in the positions we claim.

Is position important to you? Let me ask how you got your position in the first place. Paul said:

> Who makes you different from anyone else? What do you have that you did not receive? And if you did receive it, why do you boast as though you did not?
>
> —1 CORINTHIANS 4:7

When it comes to a position that you hold, you are turned back again, in a sense, to perception. Paul urges you to relax and let God show who is right:

> I do not even judge myself. My conscience is clear, but that does not make me innocent. It is the Lord who judges me....He will bring to light what is hidden in darkness and will expose the motives of men's hearts.
>
> —1 CORINTHIANS 4:3–5

Indeed, it is not simply the truth that is going to come out: the truth about you and me will come out. The day is coming when, if my attitude has been wrong, you are going to see that; I will be exposed. Be assured, you will not escape this either. You can save yourself a lot of agony if you just give up what you are holding on to now. If you are right, you will be vindicated; if not, you are going to be exposed.

But as for the position that you have—maybe it is a prestigious job or a title—remember what John the Baptist said in John 3:27: "A man can receive only what is given him from heaven." We read also in Psalm 75:6–7:

No one from the east or the west or from the desert can exalt [*promote*, KJV] a man. But it is God who judges: He brings one down, he exalts another.

Do you feel a need to hold on to what you have? Why would you want to hold on to it? If God gave it to you, can you not trust Him to keep it for you? And if He did not give it to you, do you still want it? I cannot imagine wanting to hold on to something God did not want me to have in the first place.

Remember Jesus' position—equality with God. It is important to ask yourself, *Am I equal to the job that I have? Am I equal to the position? Am I equal to the reputation?* Could it be that you have been educated beyond your intelligence? Could it be that you have been promoted to the level of incompetence?

The question that results is this: Could it be that it is the prestige you want, but you do not have the ability and are really hiding behind something you ought not to have? This is the reason you are stressed out. If you have been promoted to the level of your incompetence, why do you want to hold on to it? It is because of your pride, your ego, your self-esteem. Jesus did not see the form of God as anything He wanted to hold on to, and He let it go.

Are you emotionally fatigued? It is not God's will that you are ever emotionally fatigued. He promises, "As your days, so shall your strength be" (Deut. 33:25, NKJV). Could it be that you have overreached yourself by sheer ambition? We are told that God's way is the way of peace: "You will keep in perfect peace him whose mind is steadfast" (Isa. 26:3). If you take your eyes off God, then you will be an emotional wreck.

Paul wants his readers to be united, and there is only one way for them to have unity—and that is for each of them to let go of himself or herself. Then God's will can be united with theirs, and that would guarantee unity.

God's word to all of us is to let go of ourselves. Inner peace is better than holding on to prestige, position, or pride. Because it is the way the Bible tells us to be, it is the best way to live. It is so relaxing to know that we do not have to pretend to be what we are not. Oh, it is humbling to know that we cannot be what we would like to be. You may die a thousand deaths, but when you think about it, inner peace is better than the acclaim and the admiration.

Jesus gave it up, yet He got it back, and so will you—if it is yours. If it is not yours to have, you are a fool to hold on to it. You will lose it in the end anyway. Give it up now, and know real peace.

Chapter 3

O WHAT A MYSTERY: ABANDONING SELF-PRESERVATION

But made himself nothing . . .

—PHILIPPIANS 2:7

As we continue this study of this passage in Philippians, it is a mystery to me (and perhaps to you, too) what Paul meant when he wrote "but made himself [Jesus] nothing." What does that mean, and why would Jesus do such a thing? What can we learn from this powerful but mysterious phrase?

In this chapter we will look at two words that you will not find in either the New International Version or in the King James Version rendering of Philippians 2:7. But they are, in fact, an exact, literal, unembellished interpretation of two Greek words, *eauton ekenosen,* which should be translated "emptied himself." The New International Version reads "made himself nothing," and the King James Version reads "made himself of no reputation," which in fact is what it means. But "emptied himself" is the literal translation, and it will bear our consideration.

Paul, in issuing a call to meekness as a means of achieving unity in the body of Christ, appeals to the greatest example of all, the Lord Jesus Christ: "Let this mind be in you, which was also in

Christ Jesus." In the preceding chapter we examined the perception that Jesus Himself had in His glory as the second person of the Trinity before He became man and stressed the extraordinary fact that He did not regard such glory as something to hold on to. In the words of verse 7 we discover the decision that our Lord Jesus Christ took in eternity before He became man: we are told that He emptied Himself.

EMPTYING OF FORM

This comment is worth repeating: He did not empty Himself of deity. I referred briefly to what is known as the Kenotic theory. That is the belief that God emptied Himself, in that when Jesus was man, He was *only* a man. But that is not what Paul wrote. Very carefully he says that He was "in the form of God" (KJV) and that He emptied Himself of that form. What does that mean?

The Greek word for *form,* which is *morphe,* means "shape." With respect to Jesus, He was in the form of God, but He emptied Himself of that form, of His Godlike nature. If not, then surely God on earth would be obvious to anybody.

Imagine if someone were told at the time, "Jesus of Nazareth is God in the flesh," and someone else responded, "Well, then, point Him out to me."

"There He is."

"Which one is He? Is He that one?"

"No, that one; that's Him."

"Oh, I see. That one. God in the flesh?"

There was *nothing* spectacular about His appearance. So lackluster was it that Judas Iscariot had to single Him out for betrayal with a kiss. He said, "The one I kiss is the man" (Matt. 26:48). He did not look any different from the others.

But we may ask: what options did Jesus have as to what He could become? He could have taken on the form of an angel. The Book of Hebrews says He was made "a little lower than the angels" (Heb. 2:7). He could have been the personification of absolute wisdom, but Paul writes that God thought about that, and in His wisdom, He decided that the world through its wisdom did not know God (1 Cor. 1:21). And there are, no doubt, other ways in which God might have chosen to appear once He decided to become man.

Paul informs his readers that the decision process was twofold: first, Jesus did not regard equality with God as something to hold on to, and second, He emptied Himself. Without ceasing to be God, He nonetheless came to this earth without being recognized at the time for all that He was. In the words of Charles Wesley's immortal hymn "Hark, the Herald Angels Sing," we sing:

Veiled in flesh the Godhead see,
Hail th' incarnate Deity.

Here on earth was God in the flesh, the Son of God without an earthly father. He who was in the beginning with God is found in human form, His glory veiled.

Jesus said, "I am the gate [or door]; whoever enters through me will be saved" (John 10:9). And He spoke in Revelation 3:20 as being one who stood at the door and knocked. He said, "If anyone hears my voice and opens the door, I will come in and eat with him, and he with me."

Do you know what it is like to walk up to a room when the door is shut, but you can tell that the light is on by the sliver of brightness seen framing the door? Imagine in this case that you walk up to a door, and behind the door you think there is brilliant brightness, so bright that you dare not open the door, for fear you might be blinded. That is how it was with Jesus. Just a little bit of the glory leaked out.

COMPLETE EMPTYING

There is one theological point that must be made here. Although the emptying was not of deity, it was complete. I will explain what I mean.

The second person of the Trinity totally vacated heaven. Why is this important? It is important because, when the second person of the Trinity became man and took on flesh, He took on the form of man, which would be His *forever*. Throughout eternity, the second person of the Trinity will be God in the flesh, and we shall see Him. We are going to look at Him and actually see the nail prints in His hands. He is the only person that will be in heaven that will have a mark on His body. (See John 20:27; Luke 24:39.) All of us will be changed.

I have a little mole here on my chin. When I was seventeen years old, they took my picture for the high school yearbook, and they rubbed the mole out to make me look a little better than I am. That is the way I will look in heaven: I will not have the mole, but our Lord was not changed. He was raised as He was, and the nail scars are there.

But there is another reason that this is important, and that is there could only be one Christ. When God became man, it did not mean a deposit of 1 percent of God in the man, Jesus, which left 99 percent; or 50 percent of God was in Jesus so that there could be one other. No, since Jesus was 100 percent God, He totally vacated heaven. In that sense, we can understand what emptying Himself completely means.

Paul's chief point, however, is that Jesus, who was rich beyond compare, gave it all up.

> For you know the grace of our Lord Jesus Christ, that though he was rich, yet for your sakes he became poor, so that you through his poverty might become rich.
>
> —2 Corinthians 8:9

He gave it all up and gave up Himself, not merely to be man and to die on the cross for our sins, but to be the hidden God in human flesh.

Now, the demons knew who He was, and He had to shut them up. They cried out, "[We] know who you are—the Holy One of God" (Mark 1:24). He stilled them: "Be quiet!" (v. 25). Peter, James, and John also were given a preview showing of His glory on a mountain. (See Mark 9:2–3.) Later Paul said that Jesus was declared to be the Son of God by the resurrection of the dead. Until then it was not an open secret who Jesus was. It was only by the resurrection of the dead that He was openly declared to be the Son of God (Rom. 1:4). John has summed it up in his Gospel: "We have seen his glory, the glory of the One and Only, who came from the Father, full of grace and truth" (John 1:14).

Living the Christian Life

Paul therefore uses all this as an illustration of how the Christian life is to be lived: "Let this mind be in you, which was also in Christ Jesus." The question is: Are we carrying this out? Do we have the mind of Christ? You may ask, "How do we have the mind of Christ?" I will try to describe it.

With Jesus it involved emptying Himself of the form of glory. With us it is emptying ourselves of the form of sin, selfishness, pride, fear, and unbelief. Now Jesus had no reason that He should have done what He did, but we have every reason.

> The heart is deceitful above all things and beyond cure. Who can understand it?
>
> —JEREMIAH 17:9

We all walk around with a defaced image of God in us, and we should want to empty ourselves of anything that is sinful. As Paul put it in 2 Corinthians 7:1:

> Since we have these promises, dear friends, let us purify ourselves from everything that contaminates body and spirit, perfecting holiness out of reverence for God.

Why? In order that the ungrieved Holy Spirit may be Himself in us.

What would it mean for us, therefore, to empty ourselves? Well, surely we know what it is to be full of ourselves. Paul once said to the Corinthians (this is one of the times Paul was actually being a little sarcastic with them), "You have become rich!" (1 Cor. 4:8). Of course, he was really putting them down and rebuking them for this. Jesus said to the church in Laodicea, "You say, 'I am rich; I have acquired wealth and do not need a thing.' But you do not realize that you are wretched, pitiful, poor, blind and naked" (Rev. 3:17).

Now, what are we like when we are full of ourselves? We want to talk about ourselves rather than listen; we want to defend ourselves and do not even want to consider the possibility that we could be wrong, which makes us defensive and touchy. We feel sorry for ourselves rather than look on another person's need. We want to excuse ourselves rather than facing up to our real responsibility, which makes us critical and negative. What we have is self-preservation.

In the remainder of the chapter, I wish to focus on what I will call the abandonment of this self-preservation.

Abandonment of rights

First of all, it is an abandonment of rights. We all know our rights, or at least that we have them, don't we? We live in the "me" generation. The abundance of literature today is on self-knowledge and self-understanding. "Human rights" is a phrase that we often hear. But I Corinthians 6:19–20 says, "You are not your own; you were bought at a price." Abandonment of self-preservation means abandonment of your rights.

Jesus gave up the right to Himself (Rom. 15:3). In John 5:30 He said, "By myself I can do nothing; I judge only as I hear, and my judgment is just, for I seek not to please myself but him who sent me." He said again in John 4:34, "My food…is to do the will of him who sent me."

What does this mean for us? If Jesus did not come to do His own will, and He gave up rights to Himself, then how does this relate to us practically?

First, it means the abandonment of such things as sexual gratification outside the bonds of marriage. Hebrews 13:4 says, "Marriage should be honored by all, and the marriage bed kept pure, for God will judge the adulterer and all the sexually immoral." That also means homosexuality in practice. There is only one kind of sexual gratification that the Bible affirms, and that is within the bonds of marriage. You give up your right to yourself. You may say, "Well, I have this need. I know my rights." But you are not your own.

Second, it means that you abandon such things as material happiness outside the sovereign pleasure of God.

> Keep your lives free from the love of money and be content with what you have, because God has said, "Never will I leave you; never will I forsake you."
>
> —HEBREWS 13:5

Third, abandonment of rights means that you abandon earthly recognition except for what God ordains. Jesus asked, "How can you believe if you accept praise from one another, yet make no effort to obtain the praise that comes from the only God?" (John 5:44).

Abandonment of righteousness

Abandoning self-preservation is also linked to our righteousness, something that I touched on slightly in the previous chapter. Why do we have to give up our righteousness? We have to give it up because our natural righteousness can only condemn us. And even after we are converted, our righteousness will be the most serious impediment to our spiritual growth.

It seems that those of us who are not walking in the light will every time become self-righteous about it. We are unable to understand that our righteousness prevents the Holy Spirit from enabling us to move from Point A to Point B on the spiritual path. Our hearts are cold with the consequence that the Holy Spirit is grieved. The apostle Paul wrote:

[I want to] be found in him, not having a righteousness of my own that comes from the law, but that which is through faith in Christ—the righteousness that comes from God and is by faith.

—PHILIPPIANS 3:9

If we are to mirror Jesus, we have to give up our righteousness.

Did you ever wonder why Jesus on one occasion almost stopped a man in mid-sentence? A man came up to Jesus and said, "Good teacher, what must I do to inherit eternal life?" Jesus answered him, "Why do you call me good? No one is good—except God alone." (See Mark 10:17–18.) This is extraordinary. If Jesus is the *only* perfect person, and He is refusing to recognize righteousness in Himself, then where does that put us?

Think about this: what would people see if all your thoughts for the last seven days were flashed up on a screen? None of us have totally pure motives in anything we do. Our righteousness is as filthy rags in His sight (Isa. 64:6).

Abandonment of riches

We are told that "though [Christ] was rich, yet for [our] sakes he became poor" (2 Cor. 8:9). How, then, can this be our example as we attempt to abandon our riches, as some will say, "I'm not rich, so that leaves me out"?

Consider what God has done for you. Do you have any friends? Do you have even one friend? Do you have a place to live? Do you have a church you can attend? Do you have a minister who actually preaches the Bible? Do you have income? Then you are rich.

Then think about your own gift, a gift that nobody else has for which you can take no credit whatsoever. However, if you are full of yourself it will never be used. There is nothing that breaks my heart more as a pastor than to see how people are wasting themselves. They could be of such value to God, but because they are full of themselves, He will not use them.

Joseph had a gift of having dreams and interpreting dreams, and he flaunted the gift to his eleven brothers. He told them all that they were going to bow down before him (Gen. 37:5–11). How insensitive he was! There was nothing wrong with his gift, but there was a lot wrong with Joseph. His gift was ready; he was not. God had to deal with him. God has given you a gift, but if you flaunt it, you will have to be broken before you will be useful for God.

It is not only material things such as money and possessions that we can misuse, but consider also the wasted years of our past that we held on to because we thought they were rightfully ours. Indeed, what is going to be a sad day for many of us is when we reach a time when we finally take God seriously. Although we will have great peace, our immediate reaction will be just like a person who becomes saved later on in his or her life—"I wish I'd become a Christian much sooner."

But what about once we are Christians? For many of us, we know we are saved, we are going to heaven, but when it comes to being full of ourselves, it does not seem to bother us. I see it happen when believers finally give themselves utterly to God, and all they can think of is, "Why did I not do it sooner?" And it makes them ashamed.

I have interviewed older people, and I have asked them, "What would you do if you had your life to live over?" They can only say, "Oh, if I could, I would start at the age of twelve or fifteen and just give myself to God." If you are a young person who is playing fast and loose with the world and worldly things, who wants to see how close you can get to the world, who is not careful with your body: you are going to regret it.

We will wish we had simply relinquished long ago what we discover we cannot hold on to anyway.

Abandonment of recognition

Part of abandoning self-preservation means abandoning recognition. Jesus delayed receiving recognition of His glory until He returned to heaven. He knew He was God, and no doubt, because He was man, He was tempted to disclose who He was. When He was being spit upon, mocked, and misunderstood, He was perhaps tempted to unveil His glory, but He did not. He delayed being recognized at that time; otherwise, men would see His deity before the right time.

In fact, whenever it would appear that they saw His deity, He said, "Don't tell anybody." But are we like that? We are so anxious to get the credit for what we have done. Can we do a good work and keep quiet about it? Or do we murmur that we are the only one who does anything and that nobody helps us? Emptying yourself means letting go of yourself, letting go of recognition, and letting someone else get the credit for it.

Hollywood movie stars fight for top billing, but are you any different? Are you afraid that you will not be recognized? Perhaps nobody will notice who you are and what you have done. Are you actually saying that the honor from God alone is just not enough? Is it more important to you to have approval of men than the praise of God?

Abandonment of reputation

The King James Version translates verse 7 very aptly in respect of this last point: he "made himself of no reputation." As I stated at the beginning of the chapter, this is what "emptying himself" means. "He sits with sinners," they said of Jesus, and they were certainly right about that. What they regarded as the greatest put-down, Jesus regarded as the highest compliment. Indeed, He let people swarm Him. It did not matter what they looked like or how poor they were; they did not embarrass Him. He chose twelve disciples who could not have helped His reputation at all.

Therefore, I ask, in your choice of friends, do they need a little pedigree before you invite them for a meal? Do you have to have a certain type of friend? It is sometimes enlightening to think why we choose particular friends. Is it because they can help your status a bit? In many of our churches, are we embarrassed if the so-called middle-class structures are disintegrated before our eyes? Would that upset us? Would it upset us if the kind of people that were attracted to Jesus were attracted to us? Would that embarrass you? Jesus made Himself of no reputation, and we are to do the same.

One aspect of Jesus' ministry that relates to His relinquishment of His reputation is that He never sought to set the record straight about Himself.

> Among the crowds there was widespread whispering about him. Some said, "He is a good man." Others replied, "No, he deceives the people."
>
> —JOHN 7:12

Even when Jesus knew He was misquoted, He did not walk over and say, "Hey, wait a minute; I didn't say that. Here's what I meant to say. Let me make it right." He was not trying to be understood or to please man.

Paul said, "If I were still trying to please men, I would not be a servant of Christ" (Gal. 1:10). As long as others are looking over our shoulders to see what we are doing or saying, we will cling to our reputation. But we will not see God's best fulfilled in us. God may have to demolish our reputation before He can use us. Will you still be around if that happens?

Leave the Outcome to God

What will be the consequences if we do live like this? First, the other side of emptying yourself is trusting God for the outcome. When we let go of ourselves, we affirm God's manner of working things out. Jesus said:

> I tell you the truth, unless a kernel of wheat falls to the ground and dies, it remains only a single seed. But if it dies, it produces many seeds. The man who loves his life will lose it, while the man who hates his life in this world will keep it for eternal life.
>
> —John 12:24–25

As long as you hold on to yourself, you may not be impoverished, but you lose the fruitful outcome. Indeed the verse says that you do not even aspire to it. But when you let it go, surprise, surprise, you get it back a hundredfold! It means, therefore, that you trust God for the outcome. It many not be the way you would have done it, but remember that, as Christians, we have a loving heavenly Father who is all powerful and able to give what is best.

We are told of Abraham that "he did not waver through unbelief regarding the promise of God, but was strengthened in his faith and gave glory to God, being fully persuaded that God had power to do what he had promised" (Rom. 4:20–21). He still speaks to us.

Give up your Isaac; give up your valued possessions, your uncertain future, your ego, and your reputation, and trust God for the outcome. It will be fun to see what He does! I had no idea when I became a minister that some day I would be in London and have the high privilege of being the pastor of Westminster Chapel. But if I had taken things into my own hands, I dread to think where I would be today.

Second, having looked to God for the outcome, what is that outcome going to be? There are two things: the short term and the long term.

In the short term, there is peace and the presence of God. Jesus said, "If anyone hears my voice and opens the door, I will come in and eat with him, and he with me" (Rev. 3:20). This is a picture of peace in the presence of God. Peter advocated that you "cast all your anxiety on him because he cares for you" (1 Pet. 5:7). That is what will give you such a release within. You will know true happiness, and there will be an absence of that defensiveness that makes you miserable to live and work with, and that makes life difficult for everybody.

In the long term, there is a reward worth waiting for—to hear from the lips of God Himself, "Well done." I cannot imagine anything more wonderful than that. Could it be that one day I will hear God say to me, "RT, well done"? I will do anything for that. And so should you.

God has highly exalted Jesus, giving Him a name that is above every name. Did you know that He will do the equivalent for you? Revelation 3:9 says, "I will make them come and fall down at your feet and acknowledge that I have loved you." God wants to exalt you. He wants to use that gift within you, and He wants you to be happy. He only wants to get the credit for it. There is only one way to have true happiness, and it is His way. Does it bother you if He gets all the credit? "Whoever exalts himself will be humbled, and whoever humbles himself will be exalted" (Matt. 23:12). Then let go of yourself, empty yourself, and be filled with all the fullness of God. Leave the outcome to God, and you will know joy beyond compare.

Chapter 4

AND WASHES OUR FEET: SERVANT LEADERSHIP

Taking the very nature of a servant...

—Philippians 2:7

A Bible study group leader once asked his group, "How can you tell if you have a servant attitude?" Someone replied, "By the way you react when you are treated like one." How true! In the previous chapter we studied how abandoning self-preservation is essential if we are to become more like Christ. Now we will investigate further what it means to have a servant's heart.

Let's investigate the phrase "taking the very nature of a servant," or to maintain the theme of *form,* "took upon him the form of a servant," as the King James Version translates it. It is important to examine minutely every word as we work our way through this section because it is so rich.

What we have seen so far is this: though Jesus was indeed God, He did not regard equality with God as something to be held on to, but He emptied Himself, not of deity but of glory, and made Himself nothing. But that is not the end of the story.

What's next? After all, when you are emptied, it follows that something will fill that place. Ask yourself this question: With what was the Lord Jesus Christ filled? He emptied Himself, but He did not remain empty: something took its place.

Christ's Choice

Jesus had a number of options to choose from, both in eternity in advance of entering the womb of the Virgin Mary in Nazareth and after He was born. As we saw previously, He might have taken on the likeness of angels or become the personification of wisdom and philosophy. God, who determines history, could have chosen to enter the womb of a virgin in the royal family in Judea. Similarly, our Lord might have been born the son of a doctor, a lawyer, a politician, or an academic, but we know in fact that His father was a carpenter.

But even that was not nearly low enough on the social scale. For Paul says that Jesus emptied Himself only to be filled by taking the form of a servant. There were still options, however, that He had open to Him, with regard to being a servant. There are several kinds of a servant. As a matter of fact, there are four Greek words translated servant or minister.

One of them is *therapon*, which means "menial attendant." This word is used in Hebrews 3:5, where it says, "Moses was faithful as a servant in all God's house." Our Lord might, therefore, have taken upon Himself that kind of servanthood. Or there is another Greek word, *latria*, which is translated "service" five times in the New Testament. There is another word, *liturgos*, from which we get the word *liturgy*. It is usually translated "minister." And then there is a fourth word, *diakonoi*, from which we get the word *deacon*, which means "servant."

CHRIST THE BOND SLAVE

But there was one other word, and Paul chose it to describe Jesus' servanthood—the word *doulos*, which means "a bond slave." The ancient world knew what that meant. A *doulos* was almost lower than a man. The Greeks in particular prided themselves on their freedom. The worst category open was *doulos*.

It was a service that was not a matter of choice for the one who rendered it, but one that he had to perform whether he liked it or not. In today's society we talk about human rights, but the *doulos* in those days did not dream of having any rights. He was subject to an alien will, which was the will of his owner, and he became totally, utterly dependent upon his owner.

The *doulos* had no rights in law. He could not own property, and even his family did not belong to him. He was regarded as ethically inferior. He had no genealogy, could not trace his ancestry, and there was no possibility of controlling his destiny. The bond slave was a chattel: he was owned lock, stock, and barrel. His master could do with him as he desired. Mutilation was not uncommon, and he had no way of protecting himself.

The Lord Jesus Christ, second person in the Godhead, voluntarily chose this almost less than human category. It was the lowest strata of humanity. Jesus, who did not regard equality with God as something to be held on to, emptied Himself of all the options open and went to the bottom of the scale for the matter of existence and way of life to be embraced.

CHRIST'S SERVANTHOOD

Jesus lived a life of servanthood. He went so far as to set the ultimate example by doing the unthinkable thing of washing the disciples' feet. It was, in fact, the duty of the *doulos* to wash the feet of his owner. Yet one day Jesus took a towel and began to wash the disciples' feet, and they were horrified. Peter said, "You shall never wash my feet." But Jesus said, "Unless I wash you, you have no part with me." He went on and said to them, "Now that I, your Lord and Teacher, have washed your feet, you also should wash one another's feet. I have set you an example that you should do as I have done for you" (John 13:8, 14–15).

There are four aspects of His service that we should examine further. They are dependency, depravity, discredit, and degradation.

First, He was *dependent*. Jesus did absolutely nothing without consulting the Father first. He said in John 5:19, 30:

> I tell you the truth, the Son can do nothing by himself; he can only do what he sees his Father doing, because whatever the Father does the Son also does....By myself I can do nothing; I judge only as I hear, and my judgment is just, for I seek not to please myself but him who sent me.

This utter dependency explains, by the way, His prayer life. Have you ever been gripped by the prayer life of Jesus? Consider the following instances:

> Very early in the morning, while it was still dark, Jesus got up, left the house and went off to a solitary place, where he prayed.
> —MARK 1:35

> Jesus often withdrew to lonely places and prayed.
> —LUKE 5:16

Jesus went out to a mountainside to pray, and spent the night praying to God.

—LUKE 6:12

One of the mysteries of the Incarnation is that this Man prayed. He was God, yet He was dependent and prayed all the time.

The second aspect is that Jesus was *deprived* of the comforts of this life:

Foxes have holes and birds of the air have nests, but the Son of Man has no place to lay his head.

—MATTHEW 8:20

He who was rich became poor for our sakes. He owned no property, and everything He had was borrowed.

Third, He was *discredited*. We are told in John 7:12 that "there was widespread whispering about Him. Some said, 'He is a good man.' Others replied, 'No, he deceives the people.'" When Jesus appeared before the high priest, two witnesses said, "This fellow said, 'I am able to destroy the temple of God and rebuild it in three days'" (Matt. 26:61; cf. John 2:19). By not quoting Him exactly, these witnesses were discrediting Christ.

Fourth, He was *degraded*. In the same passage of Jesus' trial we read, "Then they spit in his face and struck him with their fists. Others slapped him" (Matt. 26:67). A slave had no protection against such abuse. In describing Jesus in this way, Paul is putting before us the mind of Christ. It was, in fact, what Jesus Himself taught His disciples. There is no contradiction between Paul's statement saying "Let this mind be in you, which was also in Christ Jesus" and what Jesus Himself actually taught. He said in the Sermon on the Mount, "I tell you, Do not resist an evil person.

If someone strikes you on the right cheek, turn to him the other also" (Matt. 5:39).

There was the time when James and John put their mother up to going to Jesus and putting in a request. She asked, "Grant that one of these two sons of mine may sit at your right and the other at your left in your kingdom." Jesus said, "You don't know what you are asking" (Matt. 20:21–22). The Gospel of Mark actually says that it was James and John who did it. It shows that they were behind it all. Joseph Ton pointed out to me once, "Jesus never condemned them for wanting greatness." He did not rebuke them for that. He rebuked them for the way in which they wanted to achieve greatness. They wanted it handed to them on a silver platter. Jesus just said, "Can you…be baptized with the baptism I am baptized with?" and they accepted that uncritically (Mark 10:38–39). They did not know what they were saying. They just said, "We can."

As we see the Gospels unfold, we begin to see the picture Jesus kept putting before them. There was the time when He advised them when invited to a wedding to sit in the lowest seat rather than the highest. Then, He said, they could be raised up rather than humiliated by assuming an exalted position for themselves to which they were not entitled (Luke 14:7–11). This is the lifestyle to which He was called. It is the lifestyle to which you and I are called as His followers and servants.

Seven Signs of a Servant

What does it mean for us to be servants? There are at least seven aspects of Christian service.

1. Subordination

Subordination means to assume a lower, inferior rank. Joseph Ton, whom I quoted earlier, told me that the first thing he does every morning when he first wakes up is to say, "Lord, I subordinate myself before You. What do You want me to do today?" Every military person knows what it means to be insubordinate, or to resist authority. The apostle Paul said, "You are not your own; you were bought at a price. Therefore honor God with your body" (1 Cor. 6:19–20). He put it like this in Romans 6:16: "Don't you know that when you offer yourselves to someone to obey him as slaves, you are slaves to the one whom you obey—whether you are slaves to sin, which leads to death, or to obedience, which leads to righteousness?" And again in 1 Corinthians 3:16, "Don't you know that you yourselves are God's temple and God's Spirit lives in you?"

This kind of talk from the apostle Paul was in the context of how to control your body, and he summarized the section that includes 1 Corinthians 9 by saying, "I make [my body] my slave" (v. 27). This is the verb form of the noun *doulos*. Paul says why he did this: "I make [my body] my slave so that after I have preached to others, I myself will not be disqualified for the prize." When he comes to the judgment, his concern is about being rejected for the prize.

2. Self-effacement

There are three things one does not expect as a servant. The first is glory, the second is glitter, and the third is grandeur. Jesus rebuked the Pharisees because when they prayed, fasted, and gave alms, they did it to be seen by men. Yet the *doulos* never expects glory. He does not expect gain or gratuity. He does not work for promotion or a pay raise. He does not think of complaining or of going on strike. It is unthinkable. It does not even enter his mind. He does not even expect to be thanked for his service.

Jesus put it like this:

> Suppose one of you had a servant plowing or looking after the sheep. Would he say to the servant when he comes in from the field, "Come along now and sit down to eat"? Would he not rather say, "Prepare my supper, get yourself ready and wait on me while I eat and drink; after that you may eat and drink"?
>
> —Luke 17:7–8

The slave has been working all day and he comes in tired, but does he get to eat? No. He now has to continue serving his master.

And then Jesus says, "Would he thank the servant because he did what he was told to do?" (v. 9).

Does the master say, "Well, this is very good of you to do. You should be tired; you have been out in the field plowing all day long. I know you are tired and hungry, and yet you have served me my meal. I do thank you for that. This is so good of you." It does not enter his mind to do that. This is what slaves are expected to do. Jesus said in Luke 17:10, "So you also, when you have done everything you were told to do, should say, 'We are unworthy servants; we have only done our duty.'" This is true self-effacement.

3. Readiness

A servant is to be always available and accessible to his owner. His master does not have to go out hunting for him. The servant should not be hard to find. There are many of us, I suspect, who have gifts and have abilities but say, "I can't do it; I'm just too committed." Or, "I have too much on my plate." Yes, we have our priorities. But how many of us are laden with gifts and abilities, but our priorities are such that we are not available for the work of God? We are thinking of ourselves, our careers, watching out for our families or our jobs. But are we ready for God's service?

A servant is also attentive. He does not have to be told continually, "You ought to be doing this." He notices things to be done and steps in. When his master changes the pattern of work, he is adaptable and adjusts to it without complaining, accepting inconveniences without opening his mouth. That is the mark of a true servant.

4. Vulnerability

The word *vulnerable* means "liable to being hurt," and this too is a mark of a servant. It involves leaving ourselves open; it means that we refuse to be defensive, making excuses. In leaving ourselves open we are forced to take off the mask by which we hope to appear better than we are to the public. Why is it that we are so afraid of being transparent and of letting people see that we are human?

Paul said, "To the weak I became weak, to win the weak...so that by all possible means I might save some" (1 Cor. 9:22). But we do not want anybody to see that we are weak. Yet when we are in the presence of God, are we not vulnerable then? Do we actually try to impress God when we are in His presence, even when we know full well that He sees right through us? I should think that we do not even consider trying to wear a mask in God's presence. We know that He sees us in our frailty and in our weakness.

Yet when we leave God's presence we try to impress the world. We take the mask off in God's presence; we put it on when we face the world. We are told that when Jesus was reviled, He did not retaliate; He left Himself open and was vulnerable.

5. Accountability

It is also part of the servant's role to be accountable. Paul said that "we will all stand before God's judgment seat" so that "each of us will give an account of himself to God" (Rom. 14:10, 12). How seriously do you take the judgment seat of Christ?

I sense among those who are in the Reformed tradition the belief that all that matters is that we are clothed with Christ's righteousness and that there will be no giving an account of ourselves as individuals because we are covered by the righteousness of Christ. You know, don't you, that the same apostle Paul who taught that we are credited with righteousness by faith also said that we will give an account, that we are going to be judged as individuals. I wonder how much peer pressure will mean then. I wonder how many of us would change our ways when we see this as literally true—we are going to stand before God and give an account.

The interesting thing is, however, that there are times when we have to give an account here below, unexpectedly, and this call to give an account can come at any time. Once Jesus gave a parable where the owner said to his steward, "Give an account of your stewardship right now." And he said, "Oh, no, I wasn't counting on this. I am in trouble. What am I going to do?" And Jesus told what he did (Luke 16:1–7). In Matthew 24:45–46 Jesus says this:

> Who then is the faithful and wise servant, whom the master has put in charge of the servants in his household to give them their food at the proper time? It will be good for that servant whose master finds him doing so when he returns.

The context is the Second Coming of Jesus, but it is also a coming of the Lord in the sense that makes us all exposed before Him.

And this accountability can come at any time.

Jesus then proceeded to give the parable of the talents. There was the one who had two talents, and he gained two more. There was one who was given five, and he gained five more. But then there was the one who buried his talent in the ground because he thought he knew God best of all. When he had to give an account of his behavior, he said, "I knew that you are sovereign, that you are just, that you are austere, so I hid the talent you gave me," thinking that was going to make God happy. But God said to him, "So, you knew what I want and you knew what I am like, did you?" He told him, "You wicked, lazy servant! So you knew that I harvest where I have not sown and gather where I have not scattered?... Take the talent from him and give it to the one who has the ten talents. For everyone who has will be given more, and he will have an abundance. Whoever does not have, even what he has will be taken from him" (Matt. 25:24–29).

This calling to give an account before God can therefore happen here below. Do you know the feeling when God just steps in and suddenly you are made to give an account? The immediate reaction is, "Oh, if I only had more time, or if I had been given notice!" We may say, "Well, I didn't have enough time." In my seminary in Louisville, Kentucky, I had a professor named Dr. Clyde Francisco. He used to say, "We all say we don't have enough time, but the truth is God gives us all enough time." God knows when to call us to account. It is up to us to be ready for that demand.

6. Humility

A servant is also ordinary. Nobody notices who he is or what he looks like. May I ask: Is it important for you to have a high profile? Is it important to you that when you go to church, everybody is aware of your presence? This is really a demand to be seen as somebody special, someone who is a bit different, someone who has something to offer. Do you really take yourself that seriously? How can you be a true servant if you are thinking yourself to be so important?

7. *Trustworthiness*

Finally, the sign of the servant is that he is one who can be trusted. My friend Joseph Ton put it like this to me: "Nothing is given to us on the basis of ownership, only stewardship." It is required among stewards that a man be found faithful. Each of us has been entrusted with a gift. You have something nobody else has. The very gift you have, when it is used at the right moment, could be the very crux of all that is happening. Your gift, used at the moment when God wants it used, can be the hinge on which everything turns. God has trusted you with it. It is yours to perfect, develop, and to use whenever you are called upon to do so.

SUCCESS

The apostle Paul said, "Though I am free and belong to no man, I make myself a slave to everyone, to win as many as possible" (1 Cor. 9:19). I will quote once again from my friend Joseph Ton, who said, "Success in the eyes of the world is how many servants you have. Success in the eyes of Jesus is how many people you serve."

God is looking for people who are willing to become servants, and we can expect that, like Jesus, we will be tested in that role to the extreme. Yet it is a great faith builder, for one who is willing to be subordinate, and all that that means, must rely increasingly on God's faithfulness. So we must ask ourselves how far we are prepared to go in our obedience. How willing are we to go in pursuit of God's standards rather than the world's, which will always be the reverse? We are told, "Let this mind be in you, which was also in Christ Jesus."

Too often when we first come to God, we are under the impression that God owes us something. We think we have bargaining power with God to ask Him questions and make Him answer us. Yet suddenly we begin to realize that we are nothing and that God owes us nothing. He owes us, if anything, a place in hell. It is at this point that we begin to say, "I subordinate myself to you."

Everybody you meet thereafter will be your superior in some sense. This is why Paul said, "Each of you should look not only to your own interests, but also to the interests of others" (Phil. 2:4). How humbling it is to accept authority from one who you think is less capable or qualified than you! How humiliating it is to be subordinate to one who you feel is inferior.

Yet the beginning of greatness is accepting authority. When the disciples asked for preferment, Jesus did not rebuke them. He just reversed the roles: let the greatest among you be the servant of the rest. This is just what Jesus did in His own life: He "emptied himself" and became a servant. He washes our feet.

What we must ask ourselves, therefore, is this: To what extent will the marks of the bond servant, which characterized Jesus' life, be ours?

Chapter 5

THE MAN WHO IS GOD

Being made in human likeness . . .

—Philippians 2:7

What is more difficult to believe—that Jesus is God, or that God became a man? One is as difficult to believe as the other; in fact, one is as impossible to believe as the other—except by the work of the Holy Spirit. This is the greatest mystery there ever was: how God became man. We must tread with great care, however, for here we are on holy ground. Just like Moses, who was tempted to see how close he could get to the burning bush, we are prevented from encroaching too far upon this mystery (Exod. 3:5).

The revelation of the Holy Spirit is this: that Jesus was God as though He were not man and that He was man as though He were not God. What I want to unfold as far as I can is what it means that Jesus was a real man and how this should affect us in our Christian living.

In this chapter and the next I am going to examine the last phrase of Philippians 2:7, where Paul writes that Jesus was "being made in human likeness."

But before we examine this important phrase further, ask yourself this question: Do you really believe that Jesus became bone of our bone and flesh of our flesh?

If you have knowledge of church history, then you will know that the first real onslaught upon the Christian faith was the ancient heresy* of Gnosticism, a belief that subtly denied Jesus' unique role as both God and man. Gnostics did not completely deny that Jesus was man; neither did some deny that Jesus was in some sense God in the flesh. What they did deny was that Jesus Christ had *come* in the flesh.

They accepted the Christian claim of Christ's deity, but they denied that Jesus of Nazareth was truly God from the Incarnation.** They wanted to say that when the Spirit, which they believed was God, descended on Jesus at His baptism, only then did He become God. In addition, they believed that the Spirit left Jesus just before He died.

The Gnostics' claim arose because they did not really believe that God could become flesh. What we must ask ourselves is, do *we* really believe it—that He became bone of our bone and flesh of our flesh? For if we are not careful, we too could become Gnostics in modern dress, finding it incomprehensible that He was really man. (Incidentally, it is as much a heresy to deny the humanity of Jesus as it is to deny His deity.)

---

* Heresy means "false doctrine."

** Incarnation refers to God becoming flesh from the moment of conception in the womb of the Virgin Mary.

The words "being made" convey an important point because heretical sects such as the Jehovah's Witnesses try to take advantage of this phrase. In the Greek it literally means "having become" or "being born in" the likeness of man. It refers not to Creation, but to the Incarnation. The Lord Jesus Christ had no creator. He was before all things, and by Him all things consist (Col. 1:17). It simply means that He entered into a new state.

What we have considered up to this point is that Jesus, the second person of the Trinity, was "in very nature God" or "in the form of God" (KJV). The reason that Paul could say that Jesus was in the form of God is because He was God. This is what we have explored in previous chapters.

But now Paul goes on and adds that Jesus was made "in human likeness." Why did Paul use the phrase "in human likeness"? The reason is, Paul simply leaves room for His divine nature, the likeness of which did not appear to men. For although Christ's human likeness to men was real, that does not say all that could have been said about who He was. The total truth of His being, the fact that He was the infinite God/man, did not appear obvious to men while He was on earth. His deity was veiled in human flesh.

Of course, had the totality of His being been apparent, then all men would have instantly seen that He was both man and God. There is a day coming when He will appear unveiled in the totality of His being. John spoke of having seen this day while in the Spirit on the Isle of Patmos:

> Then the kings of the earth, the princes, the generals, the rich, the mighty, and every slave and every free man hid in the caves

and among the rocks of the mountains. They called to the mountains and the rocks, "Fall on us and hide us from the face of him who sits on the throne and from the wrath of the Lamb! For the great day of their wrath has come, and who can stand?"

—Revelation 6:15–17

A time is coming when all shall see the unveiled deity and humanity of Jesus simultaneously. What Paul is stressing is that the Lord Jesus Christ, having emptied Himself, was made in human likeness. The reason, then, Paul could say that He was in the form of God is because He was God. Now Paul could say Jesus was in human likeness because He was also man.

The *IOTA* Controversy

Back in the fourth century, there was an argument over this same question of Jesus' deity, and it centered on one letter of the Greek alphabet: *iota*, the Greek letter *i*. It usually indicates a difference that is slight or immaterial. Yet, originally, an iota of difference was very significant indeed! For the theological controversy was this: whether Jesus was *homoousion*—which means the same *as* God, or *homoiousion*—which means *like* God. As you can see, the only difference in the word is the little iota, or *i*, stuck in there. The *iota* made Him *like* God; without it, the same *as* God.

A man by the name of Arius (the first Jehovah's Witness!) began what was known as "the Arian controversy," which said that Jesus was like God and that He was the highest of God's creation. The church was nearly swallowed up by Arianism at this time until a man named Athanasius was convicted over this. He stood alone and thundered "No!" When people said to him, "Athanasius, the world is against you," he retorted, "If the world is against

Athanasius, then Athanasius is against the world." He stood alone, but God vindicated him. His position eventually won and became the orthodox* belief.

In essence, then, Jesus was not like God, but He was God. Nevertheless, in appearance He was in the likeness of other men, because He was also a man. "Being made," therefore, refers to the natural birth of Christ. Of course, it was supernatural as Jesus had no earthly father, but it was equally natural, for the Son of God resided in Mary's womb for nine months, from conception to birth.

A Natural Upbringing

Perhaps you have noticed that "Away in a Manger," one of our beloved Christmas carols, says, "The little Lord Jesus no crying He makes." Personally, I think Jesus cried. It was the first sign of human likeness. He would have had to be nursed and fed like any baby; He would have had to be carried like any baby; He would have had to be toilet-trained like any baby; He would have had to be helped to walk and taught to speak and pronounce words. If this were not the case, then Luke 2:52 would make no sense: "Jesus grew in wisdom and stature, and in favor with God and men." If He already had these attributes, then there is no point in mentioning that He increased in them.

Jesus was also circumcised on the eighth day; He was not born circumcised. He went to school like other Jewish boys, and if they were given homework, He would have had to do it. He had to learn to read and memorize His multiplication tables (if they taught them

---

* Orthodox means "sound doctrine."

like that), and He went to the synagogue and heard the Law of Moses read like any other Jewish boy.

He had identifiable features and probably looked Middle Eastern. Yet Jesus' appearance was lackluster. Indeed, Isaiah 53:2 says, "He had no beauty or majesty to attract us to him, nothing in his appearance that we should desire him." Many commentators believe the reason Judas Iscariot betrayed Jesus with a kiss was because nobody knew which one was Jesus. He did not look any different from anyone else.

He had an identifiable accent, being a Galilean, and He had an identifiable tradition and culture: He "thought" Jewish. He had an identifiable vocation also with His training as a carpenter or, more probably, a bricklayer. No doubt that as Jesus grew up, He noticed that girls were different from boys.

We know that He was tempted in all points, just like us. He was a man, tempted just as we are, but was without sin (Heb. 4:15).

If you find this offensive, it shows that you do not believe that He was a real man. As I said, it is as much a heresy to deny Jesus' humanity as it is to deny His deity.

Jesus also knew sibling rivalry. In John 7:1–5, Jesus' brothers said to Him in a very arrogant way, "Go and show yourself. Anybody who is going to be great should go to this feast." And we are told, "Even his own brothers did not believe in him." He no doubt observed conflicts in the household; He would have had odd jobs to do around the house and probably took part in sports and games.

I am sure Jesus knew what it was to laugh; we know He knew what it was to cry. As Irenaeus put it in the second century: "He became like us, that we might become what he is."

To help us explore Jesus the man, we will examine three areas in particular: Christ's capability, consciousness, and credibility.

Christ's Capability

What capability did He have in being made in human likeness? For just as every human being is given faculties, so Christ was given faculties.

Intelligence

He was endowed with intelligence and intellect and would need to learn and be trained.

Emotions

His emotional capability included feelings. We are told that He was a man of deep feelings, "a man of sorrows, and familiar with suffering" (Isa. 53:3). He was moved with compassion when He saw the crowds; He wept with Mary and Martha at the tomb of Lazarus, their brother; and when He saw the widow of Nain, He went over to her and said, "Don't cry" (Luke 7:13). Again and again His compassion is recorded; it is a stressed feature in His personality.

Human weakness

Jesus knew what it was to be weary (John 4:6). He knew what it was to be hungry (Matt. 4:2), and He knew what it was to be thirsty (John 19:28). We are also told that He would sleep when He was tired (Matt. 8:24).

Faith

Jesus was capable, therefore, of experiencing human functions and feelings, but He was also capable of faith. Those who do not believe that Jesus had faith have not read Hebrews 2:13. It reiterates a Messianic prophecy and tells us that Jesus said, "I will put my trust in him." It is a remarkable verse.

He had perfect faith. John the Baptist said of Jesus:

For the one whom God has sent speaks the words of God; to him God gives the Spirit without limit.

—JOHN 3:34

We are the ones who have the Spirit only in measure. In Romans 12:3, Paul said:

Do not think of yourself more highly than you ought, but rather think of yourself with sober judgment, in accordance with the measure of faith God has given you.

But Jesus was not given faith "in measure." He was given perfect faith. It is hastily and falsely assumed by many that His miracles were the proof or the consequence of His deity. But this is not so. They were the consequence of His perfect faith. When He stilled the storm, He just looked at the disciples and said, "You of little faith."

On another occasion He said:

Anyone who has faith in me will do what I have been doing. He will do even greater things than these, because I am going to the Father.

—JOHN 14:12

Jesus' enemies observed His faith; even they recognized this capability. They taunted at the cross: "He trusts in God. Let God rescue him now if he wants him" (Matt. 27:43).

The second aspect of Jesus the man that I want to consider is what was His perception or outlook in being made in human likeness. Of how much was He aware?

Reliance on the Father

He was certainly aware of His dependence. Indeed, Jesus was the most dependent person who ever lived. He said in John 5:19, "The Son can do nothing by himself; he can only do what he sees his Father doing, because what the Father does the Son also does." He also said in verse 30 of the same chapter, "By myself I can do nothing." This is why He prayed more than anyone who ever lived. It is surely a challenge to us that if Jesus felt dependent on His Father and prayed so diligently, we should be crying out to God *continually*. We should have an awareness of our own weakness.

Deity

Jesus was also aware of His deity. He knew that He was the Son of God. Now at what point He became conscious of His deity is a matter of dispute among the best of theologians. Some think He was conscious of it as early as the age of twelve because of His words recorded in Luke 2:49, "I had to be in my Father's house." This is regarded by some as proof that He thought then that He was the Son of God, and it is assumed too that Mary told Him as He grew up that He had no earthly father.

Others believe that this consciousness was really only complete at His baptism when the voice came from heaven, "This is my Son, whom I love" (Matt. 3:17). I will not try to resolve this dilemma: the timing is not of great importance. What we do know is that at least from the age of thirty, He knew who He was.

Although He was conscious of His deity, however, He never tried to prove it. He hushed the demons when they shouted out, naming Him as the Son of God. The knowledge of His deity was largely kept secret until the Day of Pentecost. This could only be done because He was made in the likeness of men.

Purpose

Christ was conscious also of the reason for His incarnation and of His duty. In Matthew 5:17 He said, "Do not think I have come to abolish the Law or the Prophets; I have not come to abolish them but to fulfill them."

This sense of duty relates also to His baptism. One day Jesus joined the crowds lining up to be baptized in the river Jordan by John the Baptist. Nobody knew who He was except John the Baptist, and when Jesus was next in line, John stopped baptizing and said, "I need to be baptized by you." But Jesus refused, saying, "Let it be so now; it is proper for us to do this to fulfill all righteousness" (Matt. 3:14–15). Jesus was actually baptized for us. Ultimately, therefore, it does not matter who has gotten it right with the mode: Jesus was baptized for us. He was our substitute even in baptism.

Jesus' sense of duty is emphasized again in John 8:29: "I always do what pleases him [who sent me]." Similarly, in the Garden of Gethsemane He was driven by the knowledge of what was expected of Him and what He had set Himself to do: "Not my will, but yours be done," He prayed (Luke 22:42). It was an awareness in Him, therefore, that was alive certainly from the start of His ministry and from which He did not sway throughout.

Third, we are drawn to question, if Christ was made in human likeness, why did people believe in Him?

If you had been alive at the time, how do you know that you would have believed in Jesus? What was it about Jesus that would make another person believe in Him?

They were prepared.

Initially, it was because the people in His day were prepared. When John the Baptist came preaching repentance, people began to confess their sins, and there was a revival in Judea. People went to hear John the Baptist. Then one day, looking at Jesus, John pointed Him out as the Lamb of God, the living "sin-remover." We are told that two disciples heard John say that, and they followed Jesus (John 1:36–37).

Because John knew that he was a trailblazer, he did not try to hold on to his following. He said, "He must become greater; I must become less" (John 3:30). This is the genius of John the Baptist, if I may put it like that.

Men who are not Spirit-filled want to hold a following. They want people to follow them so that they may build their own little empire. They are so insecure they cannot take any kind of criticism or any alternative suggestion; they want a submissive following.

John the Baptist, however, as soon as he saw Jesus, said, "Look, the Lamb of God." Therefore, those who were really faithful to John showed their fidelity to John, not by following him, but by following Jesus.

This is what all of us are required to do. We are to follow Jesus, not to follow man. Any minister worth his salt will point you away from himself to Christ. If you begin to follow anybody, the closer you get, the more you begin to see the warts, the pimples, the scars, and the frailties. But if you follow Christ, He will not deceive or disappoint.

They received Him.

Those who followed Jesus, however, did so because they heeded the call. Jesus said, "He who belongs to God hears what God says. The reason you do not hear is that you do not belong to God" (John 8:47). Jesus understood that His followers were attentive to His voice and would follow Him. Their willingness to receive all that Jesus had to say was proof that they were indeed children of God.

They were won over.

But there was one other reason for following Jesus: they were won over. Jesus talked to the woman in Samaria at the well. When she left Him, she said to her friends, "Come, see a man who told me everything I ever did. Could this be the Christ?" (John 4:29). She was persuaded. Similarly, when Jesus joined Peter and some of the disciples on the boat and said, "Let down the nets for a catch," they wanted to argue. They said, "Master, we've worked hard all night and haven't caught anything," but they did as they were told and made a huge catch of fish. At this Peter was persuaded. He fell down at Jesus' knees, saying, "Go away from me, Lord; I am a sinful man!" (Luke 5:4–8). He was convicted of his sin and won over to believe in Jesus' power and ability.

REASON FOR WRITING

We must consider Paul's point in all this. Is he trying to show that he is simply sound in his doctrine of Christ by believing in the humanity of Jesus? Probably not. There is no doubt that he believed in this, yet that was not his aim. What Paul wanted to say was in the context of a call to humility. He writes, "Let this mind be in you, which was also in Christ Jesus." Immediately prior to these verses, he introduced this theme with specific rules for the follower of Christ:

> Do nothing out of selfish ambition or vain conceit, but in humility consider others better than yourselves. Each of you should look not only to your own interest, but also to the interests of others.
>
> —Philippians 2:3–4

Of course, the reason for the call to humility flowed from the general call for unity. In Philippians 1:27, Paul wrote:

> Whatever happens, conduct yourselves in a manner worthy of the gospel of Christ. Then, whether I come and see you or only hear about you in my absence, I will know that you stand firm in one spirit, contending as one man for the faith of the gospel…

Unity in the Church

What Paul wanted to see in his beloved church at Philippi (and in all churches) was unity. Yet how are we ever going to get unity?

You may say, "We will get unity when everyone sees that I've gotten it right." Well, as long as that happens, there will never be unity. If you have a church of a hundred members, there will be a hundred people each waiting to be vindicated. Yet did people think that Jesus had gotten it right?

Why did they find Him credible? As we have already seen, they had been prepared by one who pointed them to Him, they had been chosen by the Father, and they had been convicted and persuaded by the Holy Spirit.

But in taking this one step further, why should anyone believe in *your* credibility? Let us just say for the moment that you have gotten it right. You are an Athanasius of your day. Why is anyone going to believe in your credibility? Just like Jesus, it will be when someone has come along to prepare others to look to you. That "someone" is the Holy Spirit, and after He does His work, those whom God chooses to believe in you will do so.

After all, do you not believe in the sovereignty of God? Do you not believe in sovereign grace? It will not be you changing people and making them think your opinions are credible. You can stand up and give a thousand reasons why you have gotten it right, but if God does not move upon them, no change will occur. They must be persuaded by the Holy Spirit. As we say back in the hills of Kentucky, "A man convinced against his will, is of the same opinion still." As long as you try to prove you have gotten it right, you might get one or two people to agree with you, but that is not worth anything. It needs the Holy Spirit's work.

Paul was having to address a church that was already beginning to be divided, and he was calling for unity. The only way that they were going to have unity would be to understand the way God brought men to Christ, His own Son, when He was made in human likeness. His deity was veiled, but they still trusted Him, because there were those who were prepared, who were chosen by God and persuaded by the Holy Spirit.

When Jesus was made in human likeness, it meant for Him an entrance into a totally new state. You may think that you do not need to worry about this. You are already human, so you can cross that out as it does not need to be applied. But we also need to enter into a new state.

What is the old state? It is a lifestyle of pride, of fear, of unbelief, and of cowardice. It means being ruled by what people think. We need to enter into a new state: a state of humility, of willingness to lose face, of courage and trust, and of letting God exalt us in His way and in His time. God truly wants to exalt you; He exalted Jesus who had emptied Himself, and He will exalt you. There is just one condition: that you become, in ever-increasing measure, like Jesus the man.

Chapter 6

DWELLS IN HUMANITY

And being found in appearance as a man...

—Philippians 2:8

Sometimes when I seek to express some important biblical point, I worry that I will be unable to convey the essence of what I know to be in a passage. It is perhaps the feeling an artist has when he looks at his empty canvas, knowing what he wants to paint there but fearful that it will not come out as he envisages. Yet when the subject is the truth of the Word of God, the responsibility is so much greater. That is how I feel when considering the opening phrase of Philippians 2:8: "being found in appearance as a man." I want to explore what this brief part of the verse can tell us and enable us to see about Jesus the man.

We need to keep two things in mind when considering these words: what was true about Jesus when He was here, and what was Paul's overall purpose in telling us this. Now it needs to be reiterated at this point, that Paul does not tell us everything that could be said about Jesus, whether in terms of His deity or His humanity. He is making a specific point that Jesus was God but that He emptied Himself of the *appearance* of Godhood. Therefore when He was on this earth, He was seen to be a man. Nobody ever saw Jesus and then went home and said, "I saw God today." They may have said, "Come, see a man who told me everything I ever did"; "Come and see the Messiah"; or "No one ever spoke the way this man does." But He was always seen as a man. Yet we know that He was by nature in the form of God, and He *never* ceased to be fully God.

Hidden Deity

The wording of the apostle Paul here is so exact that what He is actually doing is ensuring or protecting, as it were, Jesus' deity. Jesus was *letting go* of the external glory of being God so that He was not seen to be God. His deity was veiled by human flesh.

Many people assume that it was the express purpose of Jesus on earth for men to see His deity. It was not. He only let three of His disciples see it, on one occasion, and that was on the Mount of Transfiguration, when He appeared in His glory. Then He cautioned them, "Don't tell anyone what you have seen" (Matt. 17:9). He was not here to get men to see His deity. It was something they saw when the Spirit came down on the Day of Pentecost and they were able to look back in hindsight. Then they saw that He was God in the flesh the whole time.

Paul's point here is that Jesus knew who He was, but He kept it hidden. He was God, yet He did not let people know it. We should initiate this same attitude.

Perhaps you are very aware of a gift that you have, or you are in a dispute because you are aware that you have got it right. The latter situation is very difficult: you may know that you are right. But how do you handle this? Do you need to be praised for your gift or proved that you are correct? Jesus was God, and yet He kept that hidden. Vindicating Himself was not a priority with Him; is it a priority with you?

The Vindication of Christ

Now Paul is not so interested in proving our Lord's humanity as He was to prove that Jesus lived on earth without vindicating Himself. Paul wrote to Timothy:

> Beyond all question, the mystery of godliness is great: He appeared in a body, was vindicated by the Spirit,
>
> —1 Timothy 3:16

Jesus did not wait for people to say, "Yes, we see that You are God," so He could then say, "That's right!" No, He was God, but it was hidden, and His only vindication was by the Spirit. That was what He needed; that was all He needed or wanted.

In the previous chapter I considered another of the apostle Paul's carefully worded phrases: "Being made in human likeness." We noticed how these words leave room for His deity. Similarly, the words "being found in appearance as a man" also leave room for deity. Yet make no mistake about this: Jesus was a man. On the Day of Pentecost, Peter preached:

> Men of Israel, listen to this: Jesus of Nazareth was a man accredited by God to you by miracles, wonders and signs, which God did among you through him, as you yourselves know.
>
> —Acts 2:22

Paul described Jesus as one who:

As to His human nature was a descendant of David, and who
through the Spirit was declared with power to be the Son of God
by his resurrection from the dead.

—ROMANS 1:3

Notice that the Resurrection did not make Him the Son of God:
it was merely the point of recognition for others. It is important to
look at this very carefully because people like the Gnostics, those
ancient heretics of the first and second centuries whom we met in
the previous chapter, distort the truth. They cling to the verses that
say "human likeness" and "appearance as a man" and conclude,
"Yes, He wasn't really man." The Jehovah's Witnesses take the same
phrases and say, "He wasn't really God." On the surface it would
seem to just suit their theories. The question is, therefore, if Jesus
was in the likeness of men, does it mean that He was not really man?
Similarly, if He was "found in appearance as a man," was He not
really man?

SCHEMA

There are two Greek words I want to look at in this connection.
The first is *schema*, which means "outward fashion that appeals to the
senses." It is used only on one other occasion in the New Testament,
and that is in 1 Corinthians 7:31: "This world in its present *form* is
passing away" (emphasis added).

When we come across a Greek word that is only used once or
twice in the New Testament and we are not sure of its meaning, the
only thing to do is to go back and read ancient Hellenistic literature
and see how they used the word. The way it was used then is likely
to be the way the word was generally understood.

Its usage confirms the teaching of this passage; that is, Jesus willingly adopted a certain appearance by which He was recognizable and identifiable. He did not look one way one day and another way another day. He confined Himself to an appearance that marked Him out as a man.

EURETHEIS

The word *schema* is used in this passage in conjunction with the second Greek word at which I want to look. It is *euretheis,* which means "being found," an aorist passive participle. This phrase relates to Christ in a number of ways and even is used in reference to Jesus' birth. A very similar word is used in Matthew 1:18: "His mother Mary was pledged to be married to Joseph, but before they came together, she was *found to be* with child through the Holy Spirit" (emphasis added).

BEING FOUND IN THE WOMB

What is interesting is that Jesus was found in a particular place. This is because our Lord could only be in one place at a time. He was bound by the finite and was found to be in the womb of the Virgin Mary.

The angels could look high and low throughout heaven and the universe, but there would be one place, and one place alone, where the Son of God would be found—in a maiden's womb in Nazareth.

Incidentally, we know that Jesus did not become man by inhabiting flesh made from the dust of the ground. When God made Adam, the first man, He made Adam from the dust. Yet when God became man, and the second person of the Godhead went to earth, instead of being born with the dust of the ground, God became an embryo that would grow and develop in a virgin's womb for the full gestation period of nine months. Paul wrote in Galatians 4:4, "But when the time had fully come, God sent his Son, born of a woman, born under law."

Being Found as a Man

A second area to which these Greek words refer is Jesus' being. God gave His Son total being. Now this is a subtle point, but it is of critical importance for those who are particularly concerned that the Bible teaches the deity of Christ.

A young Jewish man in my congregation visited me once, very anxious about this passage. He wanted to know whether the Greek word for "being" in verse 8 was the same word that is used in verse 6. It could be that many would not even be bothered about this, but here was a man coming from a Jewish background, knowing what the Jews say about Jesus. It was very important to him because he could see that Paul said clearly that Jesus was by nature in the form of God. This young man therefore queried, "If you have that same word 'being' coming up later in verse 8, applying to Jesus being found in appearance as a man, we would be in trouble in holding to the deity of Jesus."

The fact is that the Greek word for "to be" is not there in verse 8. It is merely the aorist passive participle of the verb "to find." He was simply "found." But this young man had pinpointed an important distinction. It forces us to ask why Paul used the word "being" back in verse 6, "Who *being* in very nature God," but in verse 8 when it comes to His humanity, he does not use that word. Instead he says that He is "*found* in appearance as a man." The reason is that Jesus was not man by *nature.*

He was God by nature; He was essentially God. The use of the phrase "being found" shows that He became a man not by nature, but by choice. By choice He was 100 percent man, having been given being. Paul refers to Jesus in 1 Corinthians 15:45 as "the last Adam." In order to redeem men, God Himself became man. He did so by starting all over again.

The first time that God made man, that is, Adam, man made a mess of things. It is worth noting that we cannot depersonalize this. When we use the word *man* we refer to ourselves. This is an understanding to which every Christian must come sooner or later. I will admit that we may not come to it the first day of our conversion; it is something we need to absorb as the Spirit reveals it to us. In the garden, Adam was our representative; in a sense, we were there. Never let yourself say, "Well, I'm not sure that that's the way I would have behaved if I had been there."

There was the need, therefore, to start all over again. The first time God made man, we sinned. The result, the Bible says, is that in Adam, all die (1 Cor. 15:22). So Jesus is that second starting point. He is called the second, or last, Adam. Now the first Adam had no parental likeness. Adam in the garden had no mother or father. He was made entirely in the image of God. You can be sure the first Adam looked exactly as God wanted man to look.

Yet what did Jesus look like? Jesus, also made in the image of God, still took on the flesh and likeness of Mary, and He no doubt resembled His mother in certain ways. He also resembled, for all I know, the first Adam, for the Son of God was a person just as Adam was, having been given "being."

The word *schema*, in ancient Hellenistic literature, has a very specific meaning of "bearing" or "demeanor." It was a word used to describe the deportment by which a man showed his mood, his actions, his place in life, or his nature. It was a word that meant the whole manner or expression of a person's being.

Thus, as Jesus was found in human likeness, so He was given a certain presence. We all have a certain demeanor or manner. We refer to a person as having a proud presence, or a regal, aristocratic, or humble presence. There is the person who goes around with stooped shoulders who feels he is not worth anything. His attitude is revealed in the way he carries himself. It refers to a person's looks, his dress, his gestures, and even the way he walks. We all have a certain way we carry ourselves, and indeed, we all reflect our cultures by the way we walk.

I will never forget the first time I noticed this indication of nationality. It was at my seminary in Louisville, Kentucky, when a British friend, actually my supervisor, Barrie White, was visiting. His walk was very distinctive, and I recognized this walk in another British friend, Jim Packer, who came to see us only a few weeks later. He walked in almost the same way, and I then began to notice that the British have a certain way they walk!

Some years ago when I was in Israel, I hired an Arab driver to take me to the Dead Sea and Jericho. We were in Jericho at a little fruit stand, eating oranges, when a bus stopped nearby; my driver indicated that the occupants were Swedish. It was a local Israeli bus, but he could tell their nationality just by looking at them. Intrigued, I checked to see if he was correct. He was. They were Swedes! "I can tell anybody," he claimed. I decided to test him, yet he proved his ability, identifying Italians, Spaniards, and Americans around us. Each time he was correct.

It is something like this distinctiveness that Paul wants to convey in these words "in appearance." Paul refers to the fact that Jesus had a certain presence, and scholars tell us that the two words together, *schema* and *euretheis*, show that Jesus could be seen and recognized by anybody. No discernment was needed to see Him.

Today, however, when we enter a place of worship, we may feel the presence of the Lord or we may not. The fact that we do not does not mean that He was not felt by someone else. It is by the Spirit that this happens.

Yet when Jesus was on earth, no particular degree of spirituality was needed to see or hear Him. They did not need any spirituality to gather that the man walking down the road was the same one they had seen preaching yesterday on the mountain. It was obvious that the man they saw was the same man who was performing miracles and teaching because they could see and recognize Him. Men recognized His profile, the sound of His voice, and this is what John referred to in his first letter:

That which was from the beginning, which we have heard, which we have seen with our eyes, which we have looked at and our hands have touched—this we proclaim concerning the Word of life.

—1 JOHN 1:1

Many years ago, I had an unforgettable experience of that Word of life. I sometimes call it my "Damascus Road" experience, and it is not an exaggeration to call it that. The fallout from that experience lasted for weeks, and perhaps even months, giving me a conscious sense in the Spirit of how real Jesus was *in the flesh*. I used to try to explain this to close friends, but they would just nod their heads and say, "Yes, well, very good." I just wanted to scream out that I had had this experience, for I could not seem to share it with anyone.

It may be that you have had this sort of thing happen to you where you have had a particular experience with the Lord, and you would just like to find one other person who would say, "I know exactly what you mean."

The nearest anyone came to understanding my experience was back in 1982 when I met a Russian man. He spoke no English, but through an interpreter he wanted to say to me, "Jesus Christ is more real to me than my own existence." I began to talk to him through the translator, and it was so thrilling. I started to put to this man certain theological points in relation to this, and he just took them and agreed with each one. It was so exciting!

I hope that in the event of revival, there will be such a sense of God that we are aware of Jesus, just as that Russian man was. This is part of what is meant by "discerning the Lord's body," as the King James Version puts it, in the Lord's Supper, although it is not the only meaning. Hebrews 13:8 says, "Jesus Christ is the same yesterday and today and forever." He had a certain presence, and this He has retained. He looks and sounds the same now as He did on earth. Just as the Holy Spirit testifies that Jesus is God, so He testifies that Jesus is man in the flesh. He has not changed. Jesus is there now in glory, bone of our bone, flesh of our flesh. There is a man in glory!

Being Found to Be Perfect

The phrase "being found in appearance as a man" refers also to Jesus' behavior. Jesus lived in the real world just as we do, which presupposes a certain behavior. He did not live in total isolation—in a cave or in a monastery. He lived openly in the world. He was a real man. And yet His behavior was impeccable, publicly and privately, at home, with the disciples, with crowds, before the Pharisees, and even before the chief priests and Pontius Pilate.

All that the first Adam was required to do was not to eat of a particular tree. The last Adam had to live without sin before God and man, every moment of His life.

His perfect behavior meant that He was sinless before women. Women were around Him all the time. Why was that? They were there because they loved Him. He respected them, and they could tell it. Why do you think that Mary Magdalene was there at the cross and His resurrection? She was a prostitute. Men had used her and made her feel cheap. Instead the Lord loved her with the respect she had never met in anyone else.

Jesus was sinless, too, before His enemies. He knew their motives; He could tell when they were taking notes and just trying to find some work that they could report. He knew they were trying to trap Him, but He could never retort or defend Himself. He could never take advantage of the resources He had as God/man to vindicate Himself right on the spot. He was not allowed to do that. He was sinless, above all, before the Father. He said, "I always do what pleases him" (John 8:29).

And if we love to please Him, we will not sin before men or God.

Finally, this phrase of Philippians 2:8 refers to Jesus' body. Jesus had a real body. Paul calls it "the likeness of sinful man" (Rom. 8:3)—not sinful man, but the *likeness* of sinful man.

It was a male body. God chose the gender, and He was to be the Son of God, circumcised on the eighth day. We must do away with this demonic nonsense that has come along that would neutralize the deity, if not make Him feminine. Jesus was found in appearance *as a man*.

It was also a body capable of all the pain, natural urges, and instincts of human nature. This is why He would get hungry, tired, and thirsty. We are told that He was "tempted in every way, just as we are—yet was without sin" (Heb. 4:15). Much of what He endured, however, went beyond what we can comprehend. In particular, the pain that He suffered in His body we will never know or experience.

We must consider, therefore, what all this has to do with us, because Paul said, "Let this mind be in *you*, which was also in Christ Jesus." Some might say, "Wait a minute; I am already in human likeness; I've been born, I have being, I have a certain presence, my behavior is my own, and I certainly have a body. I'm already there. I can skip over this section!" It is more than the mere fact that you exist; it is what you do with the fact that you have been born and *do* exist that is important.

CHOSEN BY GOD

Why did God make you *you* and not somebody else? Do you think that God misfired? Do you think that there are accidents with God? Do you not know that God had you in mind from all eternity and that He shaped you in your mother's womb, overruling every experience you knew? It is all part of God fashioning you; He has a purpose for your life, and He has given you something that is yours.

Your calling is irrevocable. This is the promise of a gift from God. It will not be something that you will lose. Something may be wrong with you, but your gift will be intact.

It is too easy to claim a false modesty in this. All of us who are in the body have been given a gift: you may be the eye, you may be the hand, or you may be the foot, but the question is, how do you use it (1 Cor. 12:14–26)? Will you make others recognize it? To put it another way, suppose that you are right about something and you know it. You could, if you wanted to, by one word spill the beans and just vindicate yourself.

But what would Jesus have done? As we have seen, Jesus was God, yet He never thrust this upon anyone. They always saw Him only as a man. He revealed His deity to Peter, James, and John on the mountain when He was transfigured before them, yet even then He told them to keep it quiet. But Jesus was vindicated by the Spirit. The Spirit's witness was enough for Him, and the Spirit's willingness to show others who Jesus was, was enough for Him. He did not need to broadcast who He was.

He was always found where and when God wanted Him. We need to be found in the same place. Just to know that we are pleasing the Father should be enough. It is upon that goal that we must set our minds.

Chapter 7

KNEELS IN HUMILITY

He humbled himself...

—Philippians 2:8

As we have been looking at this passage in some detail, we have kept in mind the reason why Paul wrote this section. The context of this passage is the call to humility. Only in answering this call does Paul know that the Philippians will enjoy unity as the body of Christ. Earlier in the passage Paul wrote, "Do nothing out of selfish ambition or vain conceit, but in humility consider others better than yourselves" (v. 3). Paul informs his readers that unity comes, not because one person is vindicated, but because all do what Jesus wants.

Have you ever noticed that the Bible never requires anything of us that the Son of God did not do Himself? The greatest hypocrisy in the world is putting demands on others that you would not do yourself. Everything that God asks of us, Jesus did on earth, yet we sometimes think when we first hear the call that it is something that we cannot bear to do because of the cost. This shows that our concern is merely with what we are going to have to relinquish and what our lifestyle would be like as a result. Indeed, that is our impulsive reaction the first time we hear any command from God.

John writes in his first letter, "This is love for God: to obey his commands. And his commands are not burdensome" (1 John 5:3). We are told that they are not heavy, yet we still think they are going to be. What we are told to do is follow God's way. Indeed, only a fool would turn his back on a request God makes.

It does not matter what the request is, whether it is to witness, to tithe, or to inconvenience ourselves in some way. That is part of God's call to humility. That is emancipation, and it is worth it all, for everything that God requires of us is followed with commensurate grace. As St. Augustine prayed, "Give what you command, and command what you will."

BEING HUMBLED FROM WITHOUT

Just as God calls us to humility, so Jesus was called. Paul tells us "he humbled himself." You may have thought that it was not necessary for Jesus to do that. You may have thought Jesus was by nature meek and mild; after all, He did say, "I am gentle and humble in heart" (Matt. 11:29). However, I think that some people have the idea that Jesus was what we in America would call "square." This is completely wrong. Jesus was a real man. He became like us; this is why the writer of Hebrews keeps talking about His humility.

> [He] was tempted in every way, just as we are—yet was without sin.
>
> —HEBREWS 4:15

> In bringing many sons to glory, it was fitting that God, for whom and through whom everything exists, should make the author of their salvation perfect through suffering.
>
> —HEBREWS 2:10

Although he was a son, he learned obedience from what he suffered.

—HEBREWS 5:8

Jesus therefore was no "square," but He showed His strength and power through what He endured. Jesus, in fact, was the most humble person that ever lived. Yet it was not a received humility; it was an achieved humility. He humbled Himself.

Why do you suppose Satan tempted Him as he did? We are told in Matthew 4 that the devil took Jesus up to a high mountain and showed Him the kingdoms of the world and the glory of them, and then offered them to Him. Why should the devil bother to tempt Him along those lines?

Thinking of our own temptations, what are you facing in your own life at this moment? Could it be that you need to humble yourself? It is not a question of having it done for you. *You* must humble yourself.

Are you a strong-willed person? Do you have a reputation for being a man's man, and you feel you have to prove your virility, your masculinity, or your authority? Letting that image be tarnished requires humility. Or perhaps you are difficult to get along with.

Conversely, the opposite may be true. You may say, "I'm not a strong-willed person; I'm a weak-willed person." Does that make you exempt? This is just another form of pride, and you too need to humble yourself. Maybe the hardest thing you ever did was to accept responsibility and assert your input. It will take humility to do it.

None of us are humble by nature. There is no such thing. Even

Jesus was not; He humbled Himself. There is a crucial difference, however, between our Lord and us in this connection. We are told that Jesus humbled Himself. In contrast, any humility that seems to flow from us is due to one thing; we have been humbled. Our humility, therefore, if you can call it that, tends to be passive; we are humbled involuntarily.

It can come, for example, from without. God sometimes allows something that brings us to our knees. It may be when our foolishness catches up with us and we are humiliated. It may be when Satan gets in and makes us do stupid things, and we are embarrassed. We may not recognize it at the time, yet what is happening to us may be nothing but God judging us.

Could it be that what you are going through is the judgment of God on you? It is painful to admit that, and yet, if it is God so working, we have the example of David to show us humility. When David saw that God was going to judge him, he said, "Let us fall into the hands of the LORD, for his mercy is great" (2 Sam. 24:14).

THORNS IN THE FLESH

I take comfort from the fact that the great apostle Paul had what he called his "thorn in the flesh." It was a messenger of Satan given "to torment me," he said, "to keep me from becoming conceited because of these surpassingly great revelations" (2 Cor. 12:7). I suspect that we all need a thorn in our flesh. Our thorn in the flesh could come in various forms: it could be misfortune, financial loss, calamity, or losing a job; it could be failure, losing face; human weakness; the inability to cope; or some ailment. It could be painful, the withholding of vindication.

Our thorn could also be embarrassment as a result of making a mistake in front of everybody. Or perhaps you are unable to answer the questions put to you by your critics, and you are made to look foolish. It even could be that you were just found out, and being a rather proud person, you were caught in your arrogance. Remember the words of Jesus in Luke 14:8–9:

> When someone invites you to a wedding feast, do not take the place of honor, for a person more distinguished than you may have been invited. If so, the host who invited both of you will come and say to you, "Give this man your seat." Then, humiliated, you will have to take the least important place.

Notice the use of the word *humiliated*. This instance shows us clearly how our arrogance can find us out.

We can feel humbled simply because we are in a situation where we are forced not to look very prosperous. Compared to others, perhaps you do not have a very nice place to live, nice clothes, or a nice vehicle. Yet that does not make you humble; that just humbles you. And here is the clincher: God can humble us, but that does not make us humble.

Often it does not do us any good. Too often what happens when God humbles us is that we rush to explain ourselves: "Perhaps I shouldn't have done that." "It really wasn't all that bad." "I wasn't at my best." Thus we waste a golden opportunity to learn to be humble.

Instead we cover ourselves, shake the dust off, and go back to normal. We were humbled, and then we excused the whole thing. In contrast, we could take what happened lying down and quietly say, "From now on I'm just going to humble myself," and begin a life of peace and freedom and a practice of the presence of God that few people know anything about. Yet that happens so seldom. Too often, being humbled does not result in us gaining any humility at all.

BEING HUMBLED FROM WITHIN

God, however, has other means of making us humble. He may humble us through a sermon, perhaps, or through a hymn. It can happen simply through our response to the actions of a friend.

We can see the effect of this humbling from within in the words of Isaiah when he glimpsed the glory of the Lord and said, "Woe to me!" (Isa. 6:5). He was truly humbled. That sense of the presence of the Lord stayed with the prophet, and this is the test of our humility.

Sometimes in a service or an emotional moment you respond to the Lord. Perhaps you go forward at the close of a meeting. At the time you are entirely sincere. You feel humbled. You think, *Lord, I'm sorry*, and you want to voice it. Going forward can sometimes do that. Yet that can be good and bad. It just might mean that you think you have paid your dues—you have gone forward. You have made your act of humility, but a week or two later it is back to business as usual.

That is what I mean when I say that humility must be *achieved*, not merely *received*. It is an active process that must become a twenty-four-hour-a-day lifestyle. We have already noted that Jesus humbled Himself, showing that He participated in the process. This comes through the Greek where the emphasis is not on the subject but on the act. What He *did* was what was important. Incidentally, this is not synonymous with *ekenosen*, the Greek phrase that we dealt with earlier, meaning "emptied Himself." It is not the same, for it was one thing for our Lord to do that in eternity; it was another thing to keep it up in time.

Look rather at the example of our Lord emptying Himself, turning His back on the glory of deity and becoming nothing and then living like that. May God grant that something similar will happen to us: that our commitment means something and takes effect in the long term. It may be that you will be the only one who lives in this way, and that can be a very lonely route to follow. But you will have peace. Like Jesus, you will be actively working at being humble just as He "humbled himself" throughout His entire life on earth, both in devotion to the Father and in acceptance of the human lot.

To be more particular, we must consider how Jesus' humility was expressed.

HUMILITY OF ATTITUDE

First, it was seen in His attitude. Before it is ever obvious, humility has to begin in your heart. We are told, "For as he thinketh in his heart, so is he" (Prov. 23:7, KJV), and "Guard your heart, for it is the wellspring of life" (Prov. 4:23). Jesus said also, in Matthew 12:34, "For out of the overflow of the heart the mouth speaks." Jesus acted as He did because He forced upon Himself a certain kind of attitude.

This is why James could write, "Everyone should be quick to listen, slow to speak and slow to become angry" (James 1:19). But how is that possible? It is because of a certain attitude. John put it in the practical terms of loving your brother. He said, "Whoever loves his brother lives in the light, and there is nothing in him to make him stumble" (1 John 2:10). The person who loves and keeps no grudges does not keep reminding his brother of a past grievance. He does not let hurtful comments slip out.

Are you like that? Do you blurt out past grievances and then cover up with excuses like, "Oh, I didn't really mean that." But ten minutes later or five days later, you do it again. The reason you do that is that you are holding a grudge. There is hatred and an inability to forgive the one who has wronged you. It is your form of punishing the offender.

But you, the one holding the grudge, are the loser. You feel impoverished and miserable. Nothing you say is right; it all sounds gloomy.

There are those who every time they open their mouth, poison just comes out. All they can think about is offense, and it dominates their speech. According to John, the remedy for this behavior is an attitude of love and total forgiveness. Only when our attitude *inside* is changed are we affected on the outside. It can easily be seen. No longer are we always making silly comments and rubbing people the wrong way. No longer do people have to walk on eggshells around us all the time.

HUMILITY MEANS ADAPTABILITY

Looking further at the example of Jesus' humility, we can see that often Jesus approached people in different ways. He had to adjust to the person to whom He was talking, to the people He had to deal with, to the place where He was at, and often to the situation. His adaptability was obvious because He accepted people as they were. This was part of Jesus' humility.

Humbling yourself, therefore, does not mean making people adjust to you; *it is making yourself adjust to them*. Satan will throw people in your path and put people around you who annoy you and get your goat, people who are foolish or not very clever. Remember that you are praying to be more like Jesus. You have somebody in front of you that Jesus would adjust to because He humbled Himself. He had to do it all the time.

Just like sheep in a field, we always think the grass is greener on the other side of the fence: "I would be happy if I were living or working elsewhere." "If only I were married to someone else." Let me tell you something; happiness in the external is fleeting. As long as you get your comfort and satisfaction because of the way the situation is, then it is only going to last until the situation changes. And it will change. Learn to find your peace internally. Then external changes will not alter it. You can be happy anywhere.

Humility Means Accountability

Did you know that Jesus was always accountable? He was the Son of God, yet He was accountable to His Father the whole time. Paul used the little phrase in Romans 15:3, "Even Christ did not please himself." Everything Jesus was doing, He was looking up to the Father, getting His approval and instructions. He said, "I seek to please...him who sent me" (John 5:30).

Now we know that we are accountable to God. We are not our own. There is also a sense in which we are accountable to each other. Both are evident when we consider some of these verses that we like to sweep under the carpet. Jesus said:

> I tell you that men will have to give an account on the day of judgment for every careless word they have spoken.
>
> —MATTHEW 12:36

What a day of embarrassment that will be! We are confronted with similar truths by the apostle Paul:

> Why do you judge your brother? Or why do you look down on your brother? For we will all stand before the judgment seat. It is written: "As surely as I live," says the Lord, "every knee will bow before me; every tongue will confess to God."
>
> —ROMANS 14:10–11

> We must all appear before the judgment seat of Christ, that each may receive what is due to him for the things done while in the body, whether good or bad.
>
> —2 CORINTHIANS 5:10

Peter speaks just as strongly about our accountability when he writes that the one who is living for God:

> …does not live the rest of his earthly life for evil human desires, but rather for the will of God. For you have spent enough time in the past doing what pagans choose to do, living in debauchery, lust, drunkenness, orgies, carousing and detestable idolatry. They think it strange that you do not plunge with them into the same flood of dissipation, they heap abuse on you. But they will have to give account to him who is ready to judge the living and the dead.
>
> —1 PETER 4:2–5

Now when this matter of accountability grips you, I guarantee you one thing—you will change. Knowledge of your accountability will change the way you live. You will watch your conduct, your attitude, and your words. For when the day of judgment comes, it is all going to be seen. At present we can put on a brave face, wear a mask, and so forth, but one day God is going to spill the beans. Everyone shall have his own praise of God, and we will be able to look at each other and know how God has judged us.

If we really believed that, we would change, but we do not like to receive verses like that. We would like to just cut them out and not have to worry about them, but this is part of our humbling ourselves—that we take all of God's Word seriously.

Jesus got His joy from pleasing the Father. It must have meant a lot to Him to hear the words at His baptism, "This is my Son, whom I love; with him I am well pleased" (Matt. 3:17). That is like a father approving of the first thirty years of his son's life in one fell swoop. What that must have meant to Him! From that point He goes on with His public ministry until, on the Mount of Transfiguration, Jesus heard the words of approval again, "This is my Son, whom I love; with him I am well pleased" (Matt. 17:5).

That is the way our Lord got His joy, and it makes me wonder, have we learned the joy of just pleasing God and getting our approval from Him? "How can you believe," we are asked, "if you accept praise from one another?" (John 5:44).

Humility Leads to Accomplishment

There is another thing about the humility of Jesus; it had a final product. Paul tells us that He humbled Himself and *became obedient.* He learned this obedience through suffering.

There is a very profound reason why Jesus had to learn obedience, and it is because Jesus is the second Adam. Paul wrote:

> For just as through the disobedience of the one man the many were made sinners, so also through the obedience of the one man the many will be made righteous.
>
> —ROMANS 5:19

The first Adam sinned by his disobedience. Jesus humbled Himself to become obedient, because if He were not obedient, then we would have no perfect substitute. We are, in fact, saved by His obedience.

All that was required of us, He did; He humbled Himself by being baptized. He humbled Himself by accepting His calling: "The Spirit of the Lord is on me because he has anointed me to preach" (Luke 4:18). He humbled Himself by preaching the truth and not backing down. He humbled Himself by going to the cross for our sins.

In all these acts of obedience it is underlined for us that Jesus did not receive humility; He accomplished it in becoming obedient. He became obedient, and that is what must happen to us, or we will be disobedient. It is an inevitable progression, but notice the order: humility leads to obedience.

HUMILITY LEADS TO AGONY

Finally, what we cannot run away from is the pain that Christ's humility *cost*. He humbled Himself and became obedient to death, even death on a cross.

Apart from the physical pain there was the agony of anticipation. Do you know what it is to live in agony because of what you dread is going to happen? Jesus experienced this.

> During the days of Jesus' life on earth, he offered up prayers and petitions with loud cries and tears to the one who could save him from death, and he was heard because of his reverent submission.
>
> —Hebrews 5:7

When you are dreading something, know that you have a Savior who understands.

Jesus' agony was also increased by the need to accept His calling and His death.

Maybe you too need to experience this agony of acceptance: you need to accept what you know you are going to have to go through, painful though it is.

> He withdrew about a stone's throw beyond them, knelt down and prayed, "Father, if you are willing, take this cup from me; yet not my will, but yours be done." An angel from heaven appeared to him and strengthened him. And being in anguish, he prayed more earnestly, and his sweat was like drops of blood falling to the ground.
>
> —Luke 22:41–44

How much this tells us of Jesus' experience of the agony of acceptance.

He humbled Himself, and as a result, He endured His disciples' misunderstanding Him, one by one. It was as though they were saying, "Count me out." This led to the agony of alienation as all the disciples forsook Him and fled. (See Matthew 26:56.)

His humility also increased the agony of acrimony: "Oh, He's a king, is He? Well, if You're a king, then we must give You a robe," and they brought a purple robe and put it on Him. And then they said, "We'll need to give Him a crown," and they gave Him a crown of thorns and shoved it into His head. And when He was hanging on the cross, they shouted, "He saved others; can't He save Himself?" His humility only intensified their mockery.

Worst of all, there was the agony of abandonment: "My God, my God, why have you forsaken me?" (Matt. 27:46). He humbled Himself and became obedient to this death, the death of the cross.

The test comes for us, of course, when we recall the words earlier in this Philippian passage: "Let this mind be in you, which was also in Christ Jesus." What God required of Jesus, He requires of us.

Jesus said, "As the Father has sent me, I am sending you" (John 20:21). If just one person would take this seriously, he might change the world. God alone knows what would happen if we all did it! What would happen to our churches? What would happen in our cities? If we would all fall on our faces, commit ourselves, and stay committed, the possibilities are endless. Remember that God requires nothing of us that He Himself did not do. All that God asks of us, Jesus already did.

So I ask this question: How will we be humbled? Incidentally, it is not a question of *whether* we are going to be humbled; it is a question of *how*. It is either how we humble ourselves or how we get humbled. Jesus said:

Everyone who exalts himself will be humbled, and he who humbles himself will be exalted.

—Luke 18:14

I cannot imagine what that exaltation will be, but I do know what Jesus' exaltation was like.

We will participate in Christ's exaltation in proportion to our participation in His humiliation. The more we give up, the more we get back; the greater the humiliation, the greater the exaltation; the greater the battle, the greater the victory. Without the cross, there is no crown. You can only win; do not turn your back on what God calls you to do, for what reward, what honor, God Himself wants to bestow on us.

Chapter 8

OBEDIENCE TO DEATH ON A CROSS

And became obedient to death—even death on a cross!

—PHILIPPIANS 2:8

In a previous chapter I recalled a question put to me by a friend of mine, Joseph Ton. He asked me, "To what degree are you prepared to be obedient? How far would you go?" In this chapter I want to look in some detail at the latter part of Philippians 2:8 and consider how far Jesus went in His obedience.

Paul said, "He humbled himself and became obedient." The Greek literally reads, "He humbled Himself, becoming obedient." This is the explanation for Jesus humbling Himself. It shows the reason for Jesus humbling Himself. Some people think that humility is the end in itself. Is it? Is humility the ultimate grace? I think there are those who just think that it is. They think, *If I can just achieve humility*, as if people will then say, "Ah, isn't he a humble person."

Humility is, in fact, the means to an end. Humility itself is not the ultimate goal; the ultimate goal is obedience to the Father. This goal can never be achieved without humbling oneself, because any obedience has to be achieved by humility.

As I have repeatedly emphasized, we cannot afford to forget Paul's reason for writing this letter. It was the unity of the body of

Christ that he was after. That is why he brought in this remarkable section. It goes back to Philippians 1 when he pleaded for the people of God to get together. That is the plea in so many churches: "How can unity come about?" Well, there is only one way, and that is when everybody is obedient. Mass obedience guarantees unity. If unity is not present, it follows that someone is not being obedient. Paul said, "Let this mind be in you," and if we would take these words seriously, I guarantee that we would discover unity in our churches.

THE ESSENCE OF HUMILITY

Unity can be achieved by showing what Jesus did. As I emphasized in the last chapter, if Jesus humbled Himself that He might become obedient, then how much more do we need to humble ourselves? At the core of Jesus' humility were three characteristics: surrender, subjection, and sustenance.

Surrender

The word *surrender* means "to yield to another"; it means "to resign" or "to relinquish." Jesus' humility was evident in His relinquishment of the form of deity. Without ceasing to be God, He came to the earth and relinquished that ingredient by which men would see that He was fully God. Jesus constantly surrendered it to the will of the Father, and He kept saying, "By myself I can do nothing" (John 5:30). He could only do what He saw the Father do. He constantly yielded Himself to the will of the Father, and in the end He yielded to the authorities. He let them take Him. He could have called ten thousand angels. He would not even have had to do that; He was God and could have struck them dead. He could have let them see who He was. But no, He yielded to the authorities. He let them take Him to crucify Him.

Subjection

This is the essence of His humility; it was surrender and it was subjection. In fact, the Greek word *hupekoos*, translated "obedience," literally means "subjection": He humbled Himself, becoming *subject*. "Even Christ did not please himself" (Rom. 15:3). You could say about Jesus that He never was His own man. Everything He did was determined by the Father (John 5:19).

We must ask ourselves, "Am I willing to subordinate myself daily to my heavenly Father? Am I willing to go before Him daily and say, 'Father, I subordinate myself to You'?" If Christ was willing, then we should be, too.

Sustenance

Jesus said, "My food...is to do the will of him who sent me and to finish his work" (John 4:34). Jesus got His strength from His obedience; it was His sustenance. That is what excited Him, just being obedient. That is where He got His joy. Similarly, what makes a Christian a consistently committed person is that he gets his joy in doing what he knows pleases the Father. When he is obedient, that is his joy.

When we are obedient, too often it is because we say, "Well, later on I'll get something out of this." But what happens is that when this is our motivation, we give up when the going gets rough; we give up if things do not work out; we want some evidence that our obedience counts for something. We must come to the place where we get our joy from obedience. Joy is the unlooked-for reward that Jesus certainly knew and was the outcome of His humility.

To return to Philippians 2:8, we find that not only was Christ obedient, but also that He became obedient *to death*. This shows not merely how long He kept at it—to death—but it shows equally the identity that He kept hidden from the world, not only until death, but also by dying. In other words, although we know that Jesus is God, He allowed Himself to be considered as other than God: He allowed Himself to have another identity in peoples' eyes.

We will sometimes use the expression "projecting an image." Everyone has an image. Sometimes it is an image we want; sometimes it is one we dislike. For example, we have a certain image of the president or first lady. Sometimes it is accurate; sometimes it is an exaggeration. What image did Jesus project (and by that we imply the image that He was willing to have)? There was one identity, and it was one that if they said it, He considered it a compliment. Do you know what it was? It was the identification as a *prophet*. In truth, Jesus is said to be prophet, priest, and king. The phrase "prophet and priest and king" in Fanny Crosby's great hymn "Praise Him! Praise Him!" comes right out of Calvin's *Institutes*. He was the first ever to say it, summarizing the role of Jesus as prophet, priest, and king.

Jesus' priesthood

Nevertheless, the priesthood of Jesus was hidden from everybody: nobody saw Jesus as a priest. First of all, He was of the tribe of Judah, so it did not cross anybody's mind that He was a priest, as only the Levites could be priests. When Jesus was raised from the dead and ascended to heaven, the writer of Hebrews said that He "was designated by God to be high priest" (Heb. 5:10). Some questioned this: "Well, how could that be? He's of the tribe of Judah." The reply was that He was of "the order of Melchizedek" (v. 10). Yet this was not seen at the time. Jesus was priest, but He did not allow that role to be seen of Himself.

Jesus' kingship

What about His kingship? The truth is that He did not make much of it. He was not at all eager to reveal the truth—that He was born king of the Jews. In Luke 23:3, Pontius Pilate said, "Are you the king of the Jews?" and in response to the direct question Jesus said, "Yes."

But He did not reveal this in terms of getting honor. His actions reveal this when He entered Jerusalem on Palm Sunday in fulfillment of the Scriptures. We are told that when Jesus came into Jerusalem on the donkey, that it was spoken of by the prophet saying, "Shout, Daughter of Jerusalem! See, your king comes to you…gentle and riding on a donkey" (Zech. 9:9).

Again it is seen in the Gospel of Luke:

Blessed is the king who comes in the name of the Lord!

—LUKE 19:38

John's account makes the same claim:

They took palm branches and went out to meet him, shouting, "Hosanna! Blessed is he who comes in the name of the Lord! Blessed is the King of Israel!"

—JOHN 12:13

In verse 16, however, we find these important words: "At first his disciples did not understand all this." Thus His kingship and His priesthood were hidden from His disciples.

Jesus the Prophet

But what about His position as a prophet? Here we find that quite the opposite is true. Notice what the people said at the end of the account in Matthew 21:

> When Jesus entered Jerusalem, the whole city was stirred and asked, "Who is this?"
>
> The crowds answered, "This is Jesus, *the prophet from Nazareth* in Galilee."
>
> —MATTHEW 21:10–11, EMPHASIS ADDED

When Jesus raised the boy from the dead after He had seen the widow in Nain weeping because of her only son, Scripture says, "They were all filled with awe and praised God. 'A great prophet has appeared among us,' they said" (Luke 7:16). This is what they said about Jesus, and He allowed it. In fact, Jesus actually said:

> In any case, I must keep going today and tomorrow and the next day—for surely no prophet can die outside Jerusalem! O Jerusalem, Jerusalem, you who kill the prophets and stone those sent to you, how often I have longed to gather your children together, as a hen gathers her chicks under her wings, but you were not willing.
>
> —LUKE 13:33–34

Jesus embraced the role of a prophet, and this is the image He conveyed. It is interesting that the one undoubted characteristic of prophets is that vindication always comes later, after death, when they get to heaven. Therefore, if you accept prophethood as your lot, you already know there will be no vindication here below; it will all be in heaven. This is what Jesus said in the Sermon on the Mount:

Blessed are you when people insult you, persecute you and falsely say all kinds of evil against you because of me. Rejoice and be glad, because great is your reward in heaven, for in the same way they persecuted the prophets who were before you.

—MATTHEW 5:11

In the Book of James we find the same lack of vindication accorded to prophets. James addresses those workers in the field who had been mistreated by rich Christians who had withheld their wages from them, and he warned them, as it were, "Look, you have a great opportunity before you. If you don't hold a grudge, you have an opportunity to be elevated to the category of prophet." (See James 5:10.) James recognized that the role of the prophet, which held the highest honor that men can have, was still one where they had to suffer without compensation. For the prophets were never popular. The false prophets were revered, but a true prophet of God was hated. The priests were popular; they were the prestigious tribe of Israel. To be a Levite was like having royal blood, but a prophet was despised.

It is ironic, however, that not only does Jesus get His vindication later in heaven, but the next generation always builds the tombs of the prophets. Indeed, they are built by those who would reject their equivalent in their own day. It is amazing how people are like this. Jesus said:

Woe to you, teacher of the law and Pharisees, you hypocrites! You build tombs for the prophets and decorate the graves of the righteous. And you say, "If we had lived in the days of our forefathers, we would not have taken part with them in shedding the blood of the prophets."

—MATTHEW 23:29–30

They claimed they were different from their fathers who killed Isaiah. Think of how Isaiah died. There is a little phrase in Hebrews 11:37 that says some prophets were sawn in two. Did you know that they took the prophet Isaiah and sawed him in two? Isaiah! Then the next generation says, "That's too bad about Isaiah. Let's honor him," and they think they are being so noble that they build a tomb for Isaiah, yet the very ones who build the tomb would reject the equivalent of Isaiah if he came in their day. They seem to hide behind the fact that they would do something for the Isaiah of yesterday.

There are many more recent examples of this hypocrisy. Martin Luther was hated, but today we say, "Ah, we are the heirs of the Reformation." George Whitefield too was hated, yet today many say, "We follow Whitefield." Similarly, it is popular today to praise Billy Bray, yet he was beneath people at the time. It is amazing how we can put people on a pedestal after they are gone and think we are being so pious.

George Whitefield was perhaps the most reviled of all. The Calvinists of his day hated him, everyday churchgoers were against him, and even John Wesley, at first, criticized him for his field preaching, which he said was too theatrical.

There was one occasion when Whitefield arranged for a trumpeter to take part in one of his open-air meetings. It is a story that his biographers want to sweep under the carpet, but it is true nevertheless. Whitefield was preaching on the Second Coming of Jesus, "In that day a great trumpet will sound," and he arranged that, on a signal from the preacher, the trumpeter, positioned across the valley and out of sight, would begin to blow.

Whitefield shouted, "Gabriel, don't come yet! Don't blow your trumpet. There are people here below that aren't ready; don't come yet." The trumpet blew, and people began to weep and to wail as if at the coming of the Lord. Can you imagine Whitefield behaving so outrageously? And yet it is safe to praise Whitefield today. Such "lapses" in memory are conveniently ignored or forgotten about.

This is the problem. Jesus was a prophet, and to be a prophet means no vindication until you are dead, and then, when you are safely out of the way, the next generation will praise you. My fellow Christians, we are called today to become prophets. Expect no recognition; do not even expect a decent burial. But great will be your reward in heaven!

THE EXTREMITY OF HUMILITY

Our verse, followed to its conclusion, reads, "He…became obedient to death—even death on a cross!" Modern translations translate it "on" the cross, but the Greek literally reads the "death of the cross," which is the translation in the King James Version. When Paul wrote this letter, everyone knew what the death of the cross was. When we think of the cruelty endured, none of us will ever know pain like the pain that Jesus experienced.

Some years ago I read an article in which a pathologist claimed to have proven how much Jesus suffered. He showed that the reason Jesus died between three to six hours after being crucified was probably due to loss of blood from the scourging He endured. This was unusual because, in those days, death by crucifixion would take three to four days. Yet Jesus died at three o'clock in the afternoon, and people wondered why. There is a divine explanation, of course, but at the human level, the only explanation is that He lost so much blood from His scourging. No doubt, this is why the Roman soldiers had to find somebody to bear His cross for Him.

When we consider the horror of the crucifixion, often it is forgotten that once a prisoner was sentenced to die on a cross, he became an open target for anybody who wanted to attack him. They could do anything to him, kick him, spit on him, say anything they wanted to him, because he was finished; he was going to die anyway. Moreover, the person who was being crucified was due no courtesy or rights. You can imagine how members of an aggrieved family who had been hurt by the prisoner would go up and kick him and do anything they wanted.

Then think how much people hated Jesus. If they had wanted to, they could have arranged a queue saying, "Let me at Him," and they could wield a whip. That is the pain that Jesus endured. Any physical suffering that we undergo will never come close to what Jesus endured. Yet if we do know any kind of pain, it ought to cause us to lower our voices. It could be that God is letting you have some kind of pain as a way of being more like Jesus. We are told, "Let this mind be in you."

The extremity of humility is also seen in the restraint that He displayed. He never retorted to the mobs, to Pontius Pilate, or to Herod, even when there were many false accusations. He could have said, "No, wait a minute; you didn't say that right." But no, He let them say what they wanted to say and let those who heard it think what they wanted to think.

Jesus did not even explain to His own followers what was happening. I wonder how much He ached inside because the Father would not let Him call Peter aside and make him understand.

I am sure that, on an earlier occasion, He would have wanted to say something to Mary and Martha. He knew that He had hurt them very deeply by staying away when Lazarus was ill. They sent for Jesus to come and heal Lazarus, but Jesus had stayed where He was, and Lazarus had died. What pain it was for Him to know what they were thinking: *He doesn't really care.*

Now again, this same Jesus who raised Lazarus from the dead is disappointing them. They are confused, but Jesus does not explain. He let them misunderstand the whole thing, and the pain He must have felt to know what they were thinking. He might have said to the Father, "Could I just explain it to them?" Yet He died alone. He never let the pain He endured force Him to disobey the Father in the least bit.

Our obedience and humility should be like that.

Earlier I asked how far we are prepared to go in our obedience. Jesus made Himself expendable for the whole kingdom of God. He humbled Himself unto death, even the death of the cross, and by doing all of this, He established a reputation that God alone could restore.

Chapter 9

WISDOM UNSEARCHABLE

Therefore God exalted him...

—PHILIPPIANS 2:9

Having considered the humility of Christ, we find now in Philippians 2:9 words that describe the reverse, namely, how He is exalted: "Therefore *God* exalted him" (emphasis added). Some may think that although the key words of verse 5, "Let this mind be in you, which was also in Christ Jesus," readily apply to verses 6–8, concerning what we read in verse 9 about Christ's exaltation, these words are no longer appropriate. Yet, this is not so. God desires our vindication as much as He desires us to humble ourselves: "Everyone who exalts himself will be humbled, and he who humbles himself will be exalted" (Luke 14:11).

We considered previously how James and John asked the Lord for a position of greatness. Remember, Jesus never rebuked His disciples for wanting greatness. He did not even rebuke them for wanting to be the greatest. What He rebuked them for was the way in which they wanted to obtain greatness. This, therefore, is the issue: How is greatness achieved? We must look for the answer in the way in which Jesus achieved greatness.

Vindication Is Revelation

First, Jesus' greatness came through His vindication. Vindication means having your name cleared of blame or suspicion. This will occur when people really understand who He is—the almighty God in human flesh. The vindication of Jesus was that what had been hidden about Him was now revealed. This is what all vindication will be like. We can only be vindicated for what we are. Vindication will not make us what we are not. It is only a revelation. Perhaps that makes us not want vindication so much after all. Maybe you think vindication is going to gloss over what you are not, and it is going to embellish what you are. You may fantasize what that will be. Yet vindication can only be a declaration of the truth. Jesus' vindication only announced what was true, and we must not expect more than that.

When was Christ vindicated?

To understand Jesus' vindication fully, we must look at when and how it came about. As we considered in the previous chapter in Jesus' identification with the role of prophet, we see clearly that it happened after He died. This may come as a shattering disappointment to think that you would have to wait until after you die to be vindicated. Well, if that is the way you look at it, that it is such a shattering disappointment, then it betrays that you conceive of this life only as being the ultimate satisfaction for having your name cleared.

If you say, "Well, if it doesn't happen in this life, it doesn't mean anything to me," that just shows your view of this life and, more particularly, of the life to come. We must remember to apply the words of Philippians 2:5, "Let this mind be in you, which was also in Christ Jesus," for Jesus had to wait until after His death.

Who vindicated Jesus?

This verse in Philippians also shows that God played a role in Jesus' vindication. Now this again may be a disappointment for some. If so, it would show that you want to vindicate yourself. You want to pull the strings or nudge the arms of people and say the things that will cause them to see it your way. Well, you can try that, but you will be frustrated if God really is with you, because God wants to do it His way.

God has words for those who want vindication more than anything in the world. In Hebrews 10:30 we read, "For we know him who said, 'It is mine to avenge; I will repay,' and again, 'The Lord will judge his people.'"

You may want to have your name cleared. You may want people to see the truth. Do you not think God wants the truth known? In Romans 12:19 we also read, "Do not take revenge, my friends, but leave room for God's wrath, for it is written: 'It is mine to avenge; I will repay,' says the Lord."

SUPREME VINDICATION

How can you describe the vindication of God? Jesus has been "highly exalted." God's vindication was therefore supreme. Some twenty times in the New Testament we have the reference to Jesus being seated at the right hand of God. This is how high Jesus was placed. He was given that seat as a sign of greatness. He could go no higher.

The King James Version translates Philippians 2:9 as, "Wherefore God also hath highly exalted him," while the New International

IMITATING CHRIST

Version translates it, "God exalted him to the highest place." The Greek word that is used here is unique in the New Testament, and what makes it even more difficult is that it is not found anywhere in ancient Hellenistic literature. This means that they are not even sure how to translate it. It is a way of Paul wanting to put the exaltation of Christ beyond that which can be conceived, the highest place.

How was Christ vindicated?

Looking at it strictly humanly, how is man sometimes vindicated? In America, the highest military honor is to be given the Congressional Medal of Honor, and the president of the United States pins it on the recipient. Nevertheless, I have never heard of any honor whereby a person was exalted to such an extent that he was told that from now on he could live in the White House.

Yet Jesus is at God's right hand. Hebrews 10:12–13 tells us what He did there once He arrived:

> When this priest had offered for all time one sacrifice for sins, he sat down at the right hand of God. Since that time he waits for his enemies to be made his footstool.

Christ is reigning in heaven, and that reign will continue "until he has put all his enemies under his feet. The last enemy to be destroyed is death" (1 Cor. 15:25–26).

This is a vindication of His kingship that, as we found in the last chapter, He did not receive or look for on earth. Only a king can reign. He was born King of the Jews, even if the Jews did not agree. When at His trial Pontius Pilate put the question "Are you the king of the Jews?" to Him, Jesus said, "Yes." But the Jews did not accept His claim. Yet now Jesus is vindicated; He reigns and receives the honor He is due.

Solid Vindication

It must also be said that the vindication of Jesus was a solid vindication. Why do I put it like that? Well, solidity was required because in this life there is the so-called vindication that is a bit hasty or premature. People rush in and say, "Ah, vindication has come." However, sometimes a person is vindicated who does not deserve it. Sometimes a person is rewarded who should not be. Sometimes an honor is given when it should be withheld, but it's because of political favors done for those in office, or because the person knows the right people. All kinds of things like that happen behind the scenes. In politics a man can win who does not deserve it, or in a courtroom a man's name could be cleared when, in fact, he is really guilty. This is clearly hasty vindication.

Speculative Vindication

There can also be speculative vindication. That is when you read vindication into the picture when it is not really there. You are looking for it all the time, and when you are looking for something really hard, you will find it. At the end of the day, the question is, were you really vindicated?

It has been to me one of the most sobering insights that we are not encouraged to believe, according to the New Testament, that any vindication will come in this life. Paul says, "Let us lower our voices." Here is the way he puts it:

> Judge nothing before the appointed time; wait till the Lord
> comes. He will bring to light whatever is hidden in darkness and

will expose the motives of men's hearts. At that time each will receive his praise from God.

—1 Corinthians 4:5

God is going to do that, and then the truth will be known. There will be no embellishment, no exaggeration, and no glossing over. The truth will be declared openly for all to see, and so any vindication in this life, therefore, must be kept in suspension and speculation. Contrary to ourselves, however, our Lord was given real vindication: it was solid. For when God does something, it is done. It was not hasty, and it was not speculative.

Surprising Vindication

There is another thing that needs to be said about the vindication of Jesus: it was a surprising vindication. I say this for two reasons. First, those closest to Jesus were actually surprised that He was raised from the dead; and two, it is surprising that they did not expect it to happen when, in fact, they should have known.

Let us look at the people who discovered that Jesus was raised from the dead. We are told that Mary Magdalene, out of whom Jesus had cast seven devils, was the first to be informed of Jesus' resurrection. Yet, on the way to the tomb to anoint the body of Jesus, she and her companions were discussing, "Who will roll the stone away?" (Mark 16:3). Obviously, they were not looking for much to have happened in the way of Jesus being raised from the dead.

Then when Mary Magdalene told it to the disciples, their reaction was that they did not believe her. Yet Jesus, from the time that Peter confessed that He was the Christ, the Son of the living God, had begun to instruct the disciples that the chief priests would betray Him, that He would be crucified, and that He would be raised on the third day.

There is something very interesting about this: the word leaked out that Jesus was going to be raised. The reason that we know this is because we are told in Matthew 27:63–64 that the chief priests and Pharisees went to Pilate and said, "We remember that while he was still alive that deceiver said, 'After three days I will rise again.' So give the order for the tomb to be made secure until the third day. Otherwise, his disciples may come and steal the body and tell the people that he has been raised from the dead." That was the reason they put the stone there and put a seal on it, which was official sanction—do not touch. Surely if the Pharisees knew of Jesus' claim, then the disciples must have known it too, although they did not take it to heart.

Sometimes the truth that we do not really believe, but that gets repeated, is taken more seriously by those for whom it was not originally intended. We see again that vindication simply reveals the truth.

Martin Luther once said that when he gets to heaven he expects to be surprised three times. First, he expects to see some there that he did not expect to see there. Second, he will miss some that he thought would be there. Third, he said the greatest surprise of all will be that he is there himself. If I could paraphrase that, I expect three surprises in heaven: The first is that there will be some whose names are cleared that I had doubts about; there will be others there who will not be vindicated and cleared. But the greatest thing of all is that if in that day I myself am not saved by fire, I can have the Lord say to me, "Well done."

Throughout most of his lifetime, Paul was never sure how it

would be with him. He said in 1 Corinthians 9:27, "I beat my body and make it my slave so that after I have preached to others, I myself will not be disqualified for the prize." The great apostle Paul had no illusions about himself. How then can we be so sure?

Paul knew that the heart is deceitful above all things and desperately wicked. Paul said that he wanted to win the prize. That was very important to him. He did not want to be a castaway, as the King James Version translates it. This is the translation of the Greek word *adokimos*, which means "rejected," "rejected for the prize," and the prize to be given to someone else.

However, just before he died, Paul wrote to Timothy and said, "I feel good about it now. 'I have fought the good fight, I have finished the race, I have kept the faith. Now there is in store for me the crown of righteousness'" (2 Tim. 4:7–8). He was close enough then that he felt he was within reach.

We must remember, however, that all vindication below is subject to change. Let no one be hasty and say, "I have been vindicated." Any vindication below should be kept in suspension and kept in speculation. Paul advised to let no one judge before the time when the Lord will come and reveal the hidden things of darkness.

Secret Vindication

The last aspect of Jesus' vindication is that it was a secret vindication. This may come as the greatest surprise of all. *Secret* was one of Calvin's favorite words; it was the chief adjective he used to describe the work of the Holy Spirit. He always talked about the secret or hidden work of the Spirit. That is what is meant here.

I recall Paul's words to Timothy:

Beyond all question, the mystery of godliness is great: He appeared in a body, was vindicated by the Spirit, was seen by angels, was preached among the nations, was believed on in the world, was taken up to glory.

—1 Timothy 3:16

Where the New International Version translates the words "vindicated by the Spirit," there was previously much confusion, for the King James Version read "justified in the Spirit." Most people had no clue what that meant. But the New International Version is much more accurate here. To be "vindicated by the Spirit" refers to the way our Lord was vindicated when He was on the earth. It was by the internal testimony of the Spirit; to use Calvin's words, "the hidden work of the Spirit." The Holy Spirit vindicated Him. It was withheld from others.

Only Jesus knew it. He was given the conscious knowledge that He was God; the Holy Spirit witnessed constantly to Him that He was God. It was secret; no one else thought it really. His deity was veiled by human flesh. There was "no beauty or majesty to attract us to him" (Isa. 53:2). There was nothing about Him that was unique in appearance. Even Judas Iscariot had to betray Him by a kiss; they did not even know which one was Jesus. We know that He was vindicated on earth by the Father when He spoke from heaven, both at His baptism and on the Mount of Transfiguration: "This is my Son, whom I love; with him I am well pleased" (Matt. 3:17; 17:5).

This continues to be the very essence of Jesus' vindication. Nothing has changed. The apostle Paul tells us in Romans 1:4 that He was "declared with power to be the Son of God by his resurrection from the dead." This does not mean that that was when He became the Son of God, but that is when He was declared to be the Son of God. Up until then it was veiled.

We may say, "But didn't they all accuse Him of being the Son of God? Isn't this why they crucified Him?" Yes, that is the truth, but we know that they did not really believe it.

Indeed, they were so anxious to get something on Him that they used His own words against Him, but they did not believe them. What they accused Him of happened to be the truth, because He *was* the Son of God, but they did not believe it. On Easter morning, therefore, He is declared to be the Son of God by His resurrection.

But who sees this? Who now comes along to vindicate Jesus? When He is raised from the dead, is it so that the Pharisees will see it? What about those who said, "We are…stoning you…because you, a mere man, claim to be God" (John 10:33)? Did Jesus go and appear to them? Did Pontius Pilate see it? Did Herod see it? Did those chief priests see it, the ones who spat on Him and mocked Him and put the purple robe on Him?

The interesting thing is that when you and I want vindication, it is always in front of certain people that we want to get the record straight. We are so anxious for these people to see it because we want to see their faces when they find out the truth. Yet who was it who was the cruelest to Jesus? It was the Pharisees; it was the legalists; it was the chief priests. But where are they on Easter morning? Jesus did not seek them out.

The only collective body to vindicate Jesus, we are told, was the angels. It says He was vindicated in the Spirit, seen by angels. God called the angels together, and they got to see what no man saw—Jesus being raised from the dead. Everybody else arrived too late. They just saw the empty tomb. Only the angels saw Jesus raised. How would you like it if your vindication were only that the angels see it?

"Well," you say, "that's not exactly what I had in mind. There is some other group of people I want there." But with Jesus, it was the angels, and what a day it was for them. One of them actually was dispatched to go down to the tomb and roll the stone away. What an honor for that angel! I wonder which one it was? The joy that Jesus got on Easter morning was that His Father exalted Him. That was what the Lord wanted.

To this very day, the only vindication Jesus gets is by the Holy Spirit. Even looking at the passage that we are considering, there are not many people in the world who agree with it. Before Easter was over, however, Jesus let the disciples in on it. Before His ascension, as many as five hundred saw it. On the Day of Pentecost there were three thousand, and a few days later, five thousand. Over the centuries, since that time it has been one person at a time seeing it. One by one! Every time a person is given faith, confesses that Jesus is Lord, and believes in his heart that God raised Him from the dead, Jesus gets vindicated again—over and over, every time a person is saved. That is how Jesus is vindicated.

"Let this mind be in you, which was also in Christ Jesus." How, then, does this verse relate to us? We must get our joy not from those who affirm us, but also from the inner testimony of the Spirit. God witnesses that His hand is on us, and there will be those who do not see it, but this is a kindness from God, unless we get our joy from what others think. It must come from Him. "How can ye believe, which receive honour one of another, and seek not the honour that cometh from God only?" (John 5:44, KJV). The only solid vindication is what God does, and He will give it at the judgment seat of Christ. Judge nothing before that time. Lower your voices; keep all vindication in suspension and speculation. One day, everybody will see the truth. Expect to be surprised how God does it and what the truth turns out to be.

COMPLETELY VINDICATED

But Jesus' vindication is the supreme vindication. He was given the highest place, and our worship throughout eternity will be, "Worthy is the Lamb, who was slain" (Rev. 5:12). That is what will give us our joy then. Do you think that you are going to get your joy by getting your name cleared? I do not say that there is not going to be some joy there, for the Lord promised it, but that will seem as nothing compared to the joy we are all going to have in worshiping Him, who came to this earth, who lived among men. He died on the cross, and nobody understood it. He was raised from the dead and, still to this moment, awaits the vindication He will have in the last day when every knee shall bow before Him.

We shall also bow, and whatever vindication we may have, whatever reward, whatever crown, we shall cast our crowns before Him. If that will be what will give us joy, then may it give us joy now, for this is our Lord's day of vindication. What the world will eventually see, we see now. We must worship Him, worship Him with all our hearts, and know that this is His day.

My first recollection of the phrase "Let this mind be in you, which was also in Christ Jesus," as best as I can remember, was in either February or March 1956. The exact month does not matter, but it was a critical time for me in my life during those months.

I heard a sermon on Philippians 2:5 that would shake my life for a long time, or so it seemed. In the sermon the preacher made the point that Jesus became the lowest possible shame. And he kept stressing, "Let this mind be in you." I cannot say whether anyone in the audience got it, but I did, and I was so gripped that I went to my knees. I prayed this prayer, and I meant it: "Lord, make me the lowest possible shame for Your glory."

I do not want to affirm that the Holy Spirit led me to pray these words. It could be that I was driven by emotion or pseudo-guilt. Things like that can happen listening to a powerful preacher. Whether that was the case with me, I do not know. Yet within three months I heard my own family actually say to me, "You are a shame; you are a disgrace to the family."

Let me explain what happened. Several months before I had been baptized by the Holy Spirit, and Jesus Christ became more real to me then than anybody around me. But what I did not know was that experience was going to pave the way for the greatest suffering that I could ever have imagined. I do not intend to reveal what took place, but my reason for referring to that experience, when my family rejected me (they still loved me but were horrified at what had happened), is that the subject of vindication became dear to me. It is a theme I have in my ministry to this day. I realized that some day I would be vindicated.

THE PAIN OF BEING MISUNDERSTOOD

As we have seen, vindication means simply to have your name cleared. You have been misunderstood, and it hurts. You feel in your heart that you are right, but no one else thinks it. It is a very painful thing. In fact, I do not know that there is anything more painful, and if you want vindication, it is a very real desire. I suspect that there is no one around who does not have something in their background, some area of their life where they have been misunderstood or hurt. They just want to have their name cleared in the eyes of maybe one or two.

Here is the good news: God wants to vindicate us. Here is the bad news: it has to be done His way and in His time. First Peter 5:6 confirms this: "Humble yourselves, therefore, under God's mighty hand, that he may lift you up in due time."

In the remainder of this chapter, I will look more deeply at our Lord's own vindication, but always with our eyes on the phrase that introduces this sublime section: "Let this mind be in you, which was also in Christ Jesus."

As we have considered that our vindication is to be similar to that of Jesus, we discovered that there is no guarantee that vindication will come in this life. I personally have searched the Bible for an absolute promise that vindication will come earlier, and I think if there were one, I would have found it. Sometimes God will clear a man's name in advance of the judgment seat of Christ. That is His sovereign prerogative. But He may want to continue using you while still letting some people question your service. You may have to live with that.

Remember, Joseph was falsely accused of sexual advances toward Potiphar's wife. Are you aware that Joseph's name was never cleared? You may say, "Well, it must have been. He was prime minister of Egypt; they just bypassed all of that." Pharaoh could see that he was the man that he wanted, and he elevated Joseph. I am sure that there were people who recalled the accusations when Joseph was promoted.

The Bible does not say that his name was ever cleared, but God still went ahead and used him. No doubt Joseph would have wanted his name cleared.

You may have a similar experience. But God might just want to use you and let this aspect be left as a sore spot in your life to keep you humble. In 1 Corinthians 4:3–5 Paul says:

> I care very little if I am judged by you or by any human court; indeed, I do not even judge myself. [That is a word that literally means, "I do not vindicate myself."] My conscience is clear, but that does not make me innocent [or vindicated]. It is the Lord who judges [vindicates] me. Therefore judge nothing before the appointed time; wait till the Lord comes. He will bring to light what is hidden in darkness and will expose the motives of men's hearts. At that time each will receive his praise from God.

Our mind-set has to be that there is no promise of vindication in this life.

Do not judge.

James speaks out clearly about judging others:

> Brothers, do not slander one another. Anyone who speaks against his brother or judges him speaks against the law and judges it. When you judge the law, you are not keeping it, but sitting in judgment on it. There is only one Lawgiver and Judge, the one who is able to save and to destroy. But you—who are you to judge your neighbor?
>
> —JAMES 4:11–12

I have referred to these verses for this reason: the inevitable consequence when anyone is looking for vindication is for that person to start judging people. Such an attitude is a blatant sin against the words of Jesus: "Do not judge, or you too will be judged" (Matt. 7:1). Is it not amazing how each of us thinks that we are the exception to that verse?

Two humbling considerations flow from this realization. When we are wrong in our judgment, the person we are judging will be the one whom God will vindicate. Or even more serious, if you decide to judge another person and take things into your own hands, it may be that God will just let you do that because that person may need to be judged, and God may use you as the instrument. But you will not do it nearly as completely as God would do it. Instead, then, leave others in God's hands and look after yourself; no judging allowed.

Avoid self-pity.

This leads us to remember to stop vindicating ourselves. If there is no vindication to be had in this life, self-pity is useless. We must get out of that abyss, for it is just as absorbing as looking for vindication itself, and it is one of Satan's favorite means of distracting us from the Lord.

Earlier we considered, with relation to ourselves, that vindication is merely the revelation of truth. When we consider Jesus' vindication in this light, we see that God's exaltation of Him was simply to restore Him to the level that He had always deserved. He was brought back to His original position. Our vindication, therefore, will be nothing more than the truth. It is the revelation of what we really were, what we really did, and what actually did happen to us. There are three areas in which this revelation of the truth might apply for each of us.

Vindication of Our Gifts

God has given to each of us different gifts. In the context of using our God-given gifts, Paul writes in Romans 12:3, "Do not think of yourself more highly than you ought." Have we tried to embellish our gifts? You may be claiming your gift to be one thing when it is another. While it is humbling to accept that what you have is a gift from God, it is even more humbling to realize that there are limits to your gift. If you claim to have a gift that you do not possess, the truth of what you really have will find you blushing when it comes to light.

Vindication of Our Spirituality

Revelation of the truth is also true with regards to grace and spirituality. We may have found ourselves facing a trial and asked, "How did I respond to the trial? Did I honor God or not? Did I love those in opposition to me or not?"

Whatever it seemed on the surface, vindication means that our motivation will be seen for what it was, whether what we manifested was the fruit of the Spirit or a pretense at trying to look spiritual. When we stand before the judgment seat of Christ, our behavior will be shown for what it was. It would be better if we just did not pretend now. We are what we are by the grace of God. Why do we have to put on a show of spirituality? God never asks us to overclaim or pretend.

It is similar with regard to guidance. It is only a matter of time before we find out if we were truly guided or not. I can claim to be guided by the Holy Spirit, yet when vindication day comes, it may be found to be otherwise. Vindication may reveal that I took things into my own hands, and, although I was claiming God's guidance, it was all worthless because I was not guided by God.

Vindication is not only the revelation of the truth in terms of what I was and what I did; it will be a revelation of what actually happened. We have considered the pain of others misunderstanding us, but when vindication comes, it will be revealed whether they really did mistreat us or not.

Were they right to do what they did? Maybe they were. If so, they will be vindicated. If they were wrong to do what they did, then we will be vindicated. We also need to ask whether we would have been any different from them if we had been in their situation, for the answer to this will also come out, unfortunately. If so, why should they be judged? It will come out. It will all be there in black and white.

Vindication of Our Reward

Third, our recompense at the judgment will correspond to the degree of trials that we have endured. Jesus displayed the extremes of trial and of reward. He went as low as it was possible to go, in terms of suffering, which was so much greater having come from such an exalted position originally, and He also received the highest possible reward.

How do we compare to this standard? Our problem is that we always overestimate our sorrow. We want to claim that our trial was so great and so awful that we must therefore qualify for a highly exalted position. Two things go into God's computer: intensity and time. In other words, how deep was the suffering, and how long did it last? God is a righteous judge. If you are going through extreme suffering, and if it is lasting a long time, the greater your reward will be. If your trials are minimal, then your exaltation will be in proportion to what things really were. But this will remain unknown until the judgment.

Refer all things, therefore, to the last day, when the truth will be revealed and every person will have the praise of God. That is all that really matters. Indeed, what God thinks is all that matters now.

Chapter 10

LIFTS OUR HUMANITY

To the highest place . . .

—PHILIPPIANS 2:9

In the previous chapter we considered some of the ways in which we can approach trials and the way we should respond to them. When we consider some of the trials that face us from time to time, it can seem as if they will never end. The devil makes the most of it, and he will try to bring you down all the more by making you think it is never going to end and that you may just as well give in.

It may seem strange to begin a chapter entitled "Lifts Our Humanity" by looking at trials, but the fact is that the words of Philippians 2:9, "Therefore God exalted him to the highest place," give new hope in these situations when we are at the end of our rope. For there comes a time when the trial ends. There comes a moment when God says, "You can't take anymore." The life of Jesus demonstrates this. It can be seen as one continuous temptation, one continuous trial, but it ended. Now He has been exalted.

You may conclude from this that if you are in a trial, the only way it will end is when you die. That, however, would not be true, and there is something to be seen in this text that is most thrilling. God knows how much you can bear, and you do not have to wait until you die to know a certain kind of exaltation. God exalted Jesus, and God will exalt you even without your dying, though possibly not in the way that you want.

Joy in Hardship

Words in Hebrews 12:2 help to illuminate the passage we are considering. The writer says that Jesus "for the joy set before him endured the cross, scorning its shame." God is telling us that He has a way of giving to all of us something to look forward to. When you have something to look forward to, you can endure the present. Jesus, as a man, did not enjoy the shame and the suffering, but He did have something to look forward to. It was the "joy set before Him." Indeed, it was a kind of joy that He knew would be so marvelous and so wonderful that He was able to endure the trial.

For us, therefore, whatever trial we are in, God wants us to know that there is something to look forward to. Sometimes when a situation seems bleak and we dare not even tell anyone about it, we feel that there is nothing to look forward to. Perhaps you have a particular problem; no one would understand, and you just want to throw in the towel. Well, this message is for you. It is interesting that the passage in Philippians 2 is so much like Hebrews 12:2, in that it goes from the death of Christ to His ascension. There is no explicit reference in either passage to the resurrection of Jesus. We have the death of Jesus, and the next stage described is His passing into the heavens to be seated at the right hand of God. His resurrection is taken for granted.

There is also another interesting aspect about the Philippian verses in particular. Paul, in Philippians 2, mentions Christ's death, but not the atonement. He also mentions Christ's ascension, but not

His intercession. Now the doctrine of justification comes later in Philippians 3, but the passage in Philippians 2 does not really deal with the atonement. It is implied, but it is not explicitly pointed out. Instead, Paul's point is to see the examples of our Lord Jesus Christ, and that too is the writer of Hebrews' point in the second verse of chapter 12.

That which can be true of us that was true of Jesus Philippians 2 and Hebrews 12 make clear. We cannot be like Jesus in atoning for sin, but we do have Jesus as our example. It shows us that what was true of Jesus can be true of us, that we can imitate emptying ourselves, becoming servants, becoming obedient, and bearing the cross. It is equally true that if we bear the cross, we will have an exaltation.

But in this chapter I want us to see yet another aspect of our Lord's vindication and, in particular, His joy.

Jesus' Joy

Jesus was a person; He was an individual, and He Himself experienced supreme joy. I will not even bother to try and convey the joy He felt; I would not know what it is. All we can imagine is only a vague idea of the personal joy Jesus experienced when He was welcomed back to heaven and sat down at the right hand of God.

This has to do with what we earlier saw as the hidden nature of our Lord's vindication. It was hidden because nobody saw it. I knew a young man who was severely mistreated by his father. If you knew the whole story, it would break your heart. This young man really hated his father. When his mother died, he had to live with his father, but it happened that somebody who had a little money took an interest in the young man and said, "Look, you can come and live with us. We'll send you to a public school." That is exactly what happened. He left his father's home and went to a very prestigious public school in the south of England.

He would come to our house now and then, and do you know, he was a different boy altogether. At one time you would have said there was no hope for a boy like that. But now he was developing a certain poise and mannerisms, his tone of voice changed, and in addition, he was doing well in school. He would say to us, "I'm doing this to let my father see what I can do. I just live for the day when I can go to my father and say, 'Look at me now.'"

His father had said that he would never amount to anything. The boy had the biggest inferiority complex, and he lived for one thing, to be a success so his father would notice. When the boy's father died, the boy lost his motivation. He left school and went back to all his old ways. It was so sad.

Don't you see? This boy knew nothing of an internal joy from pleasing his heavenly Father. If the kind of vindication you are wanting is for some person on earth to notice you, you have it all wrong.

Exalted to the Highest Place

When Jesus ascended to heaven, it was His coronation day. Down below, one hundred twenty people were waiting in Jerusalem, waiting for power to come on them. They waited, we believe, according to Acts, for ten days. What was going on in heaven during that time? Jesus was being exalted, and it seems to have lasted as long as ten earthly days.

This phrase "highly exalted" (as the King James Version translates it) is very interesting. It is used only here in the New

Testament and is not found in classic Hellenistic literature, which means we cannot see how else it was used. It is a unique word, and no one is certain how to translate it. It is found, however, in the Septuagint, which is the Greek translation of the Hebrew Old Testament. One example of this is in Psalm 97:9 where it says, "For you, O LORD [this is reference to Yahweh, Jehovah], are the Most High over all the earth; you are *exalted* far above all gods" (emphasis added). It is used also in Daniel 4:34, "At the end of that time, I, Nebuchadnezzar, *raised* my eyes toward heaven, and my sanity was restored" (emphasis added). These usages shed some light on the heights to which God raised His Son.

THE JOY OF GOD'S PLEASURE

The joy took place between Father and Son when the Father said, "Well done. Sit at My right hand until I make Your enemies a footstool for Your feet."

The phrase "right hand" specifically means "equality with." Before the Incarnation, the glory that Jesus had was equality with God, but in His preincarnate state, He was simply known as the Logos, the Word. It was almost a nameless expression for the being of our preincarnate Lord. However, now that He has ascended to heaven, He has a name: Jesus.

And as I have said, I suspect that the angels saw it because 1 Timothy 3:16 says that He was "seen by angels," and for all I know, the sainted dead saw it. I cannot prove that. But those below did not discover it for ten days until, on the Day of Pentecost when the Spirit came down, they saw it, and by faith Peter ended his sermon, "God has made this Jesus, whom you crucified, both Lord and Christ" (Acts 2:36).

More than two thousand years later, if I am right that Jesus is coming soon, the whole world will see it, though in the meantime, it has been hidden. Today we see it by faith; by sight it was something that took place between the Father and the Son. Not having anyone else see it, therefore, was the joy of our Lord Jesus Christ. Recall the words of Paul again: "Let this mind be in you, which was also in Christ Jesus."

As He did for Jesus, God wants to bring us to the place where the joy we anticipate, the joy we visualize when the trial is over, is God's pleasure alone. We read in the Bible that we have a jealous God. Maybe you have not experienced that; maybe you have not discovered that God is jealous. You may not think it is a very attractive quality, yet this is just the way He is; He is jealous. He wants all of you, and He wants you to want Him and nobody else. That is just the way He is.

God's Verdict

In anticipation of the Day of days, it may be that God comes to us in cycles. I will explain what I mean. God gives a coronation day here below, which is a foretaste of the Day of days. I first saw this truth many years ago when I studied the Book of James, in particular James 1:12, "Blessed is the man who perseveres under trial, because when he has stood the test, he will receive the crown of life that God has promised to those who love him."

What I saw then is clearly in the Greek: the temptations come in cycles, as do crowns. Our coronation day here below is at intervals. Whenever we pass the test, when a trial is over, God gives us a report card. He lets us know the results of our exam, whether we have passed or failed. If we pass the test, God tells us, and He says,

"Well done." And when we feel He is blessing us and approving of us, there is no greater joy in the world. This is not for anybody else to know; it is not for anybody else to see. It is strictly private, between God and us alone. When we hear Him say, "Well done," the joy that comes from those words is inexpressible. It is an internal victory, and it can be called an internal vindication.

Jesus experienced this on earth. In the accounts of Jesus' temptation (Matt. 4:11; Luke 4:13), the writers, when it was over, record that the devil departed for a season, and the angels came and ministered to Him. God knows how much we can bear. If, unlike Jesus, we do not dignify the trial, the trial will end. Dignifying the trial does not hasten its end, or not dignifying the trial does not mean that it is going to last longer, because all trials have their time limit. God knows how much you can bear. Yet when the trial is over, and you, as it were, sat the examination, you may not have passed. It ended, and you may just have a feeling of relief. You are glad it is over, but you are no better off, for you did not dignify it, and you received no blessing from God. But because it is over, you must consider what God thought about you and your conduct while the trial was going on. It is something private between you and Him.

INTERNAL VINDICATION

We can receive three different types of vindication: internal, external, and terminal. But internal vindication is what results in knowing the joy of the Lord here and now. Internal vindication is when God and you alone know the situation, and that keeps you going. External vindication is when others see it, and terminal vindication is your reward in heaven.

Internal vindication is the joy of the Lord. It is not the joy of people, which is external; it is not the joy of things, which is external. The joy of the Lord is internal, and nobody knows but you. This is what God wants you to experience: an internal vindication. God does you a great favor to let nobody else know, because if somebody else knows, then you have lost it, and you will not enjoy the Lord's blessings. Internal vindication is when God witnesses to you, and when that happens, you will be able to face anything. This is why we have these words in Nehemiah 8:10, "The joy of the LORD is your strength." Our joy is knowing His joy of us.

Passing the Test

I have used the expression "dignifying the trial" in this chapter, and what it means is partly this: refusing to complain, inwardly or outwardly, because God knows whether or not you are complaining. How you react to the trial you now have will determine whether you pass the test and hear God say, "Well done." Jesus passed many tests in His earthly life before He came to the final one, but along the way as He would pass tests, He would get the word from the Father, "You are My Son whom I love; with You I am well pleased."

That is what kept the Lord Jesus going. He actually had joy all along. Did you know that? It was not just the joy that was set before Him. He said in John 15:11, "I have told you this so that my joy may be in you and that your joy may be complete." And He said in John 17:13, "I am coming to you now, but I say these things while I am still in the world, so that they may have the full measure of my joy within them." All of us who have sat through exams of any sort know that sometimes you have to retake an exam or its equivalent. That is the way it is in this world. Only the very clever avoid this.

But in the kingdom of God it is not that way. Intellectual aptitude has nothing to do with it. Neither has social standing or class or any other worldly consideration. All Christians can go to the university of the Holy Spirit. The difficulty is that some have not even passed grammar school. They come up to a certain level, and they blow it. Why?

They complained all the way through. They could not resist murmuring; they could not resist judging somebody, or gossiping, or holding a grudge. God gives them a trial on a silver platter, yet when it ends, they are still the same. But Jesus went straight through to the finals, because He never sinned along the way. He did it all in thirty-three years. God gives most of us more time than that. Threescore and ten is the average—time enough for us to pass the tests that He sets before us.

The Goal of Trials

What God wants us to learn is to "desire only the joy of the Lord." As long as we are looking over our shoulder, we have not reached the goal; as long as we are looking over our shoulder, we have not passed. The goal of trials is to look to Jesus (Heb. 12:2). This happens when you are shut off from all here below so that only God knows.

As long as you envisage external vindication below, it is your hint that you are not ready yet. Are you like that young man who just wanted to be vindicated before his father, and then when his father died, he had nothing else to live for? God is a jealous God, and He wants you to enjoy Him alone.

Sometimes I say to my wife, "Let's go out for a meal. Let's go to a restaurant."

"Fine," she says.

Then I ask, "Whom shall we take with us?"

"Don't you just want to be with me?" she asks.

That is what God is saying, and Jesus responded in getting His joy from the Father alone.

If this is your pattern, I will tell you what it will mean. It will mean that your best and closest friends may not understand. It was a trial for Jesus that He could not explain to the disciples all that He was up to. Yet His joy was internal, and when you begin to react to criticism and praise in much the same way, you are beginning to get free. When you begin to react to criticism and praise without taking either seriously, that signifies that you are passing the tests as Jesus did. The goal of trial is contentment with the glory that comes from God only.

A friend, Jon Bush, asked me once in connection with this, "Is it that ambition takes us so far and the glory of the Lord the rest of the way?" I agreed with him.

The ambition that makes a person want to do something has to be transferred into the glory of the Lord. Again, the fear that drives a person to faith must be transformed into that which casts out fear—love. God wants people to be completely sold out for His glory. Ambition must go so that the glory of the Lord is foremost. The goal is reached when our ambition dissolves and all we want is for Him to say, "Good. Well done."

God's Plan

When you consider the joy of the Lord, it is worth considering what God has in mind for you and what you will fulfill. God has a goal for you; He has a plan for your life. Sometimes I wonder if there may be Plan A and then Plan B. (I would not push this too far, as it is a bit speculative, but is an idea of mine.)

Plan A is what God initially wants; Plan B is His second choice. Plan B is what I must make the most of if I miss Plan A. Indeed, I think this is the way it was with Israel. Plan A said God did not want Israel to have a king, but Plan B came into action instead, and from then on it worked out. That is what God owned from then on. Maybe the problem is that we all miss Plan A. Maybe we are all in Plan B.

There is quite a hint of that in the words of Paul: "We know that in all things God works for the good of those who love him, who have been called according to his purpose" (Rom. 8:28). Yet having said that, I will be as candid as I know how to be; I do not want to get to heaven and discover that I missed the prize. I think Paul felt that way. He said, "I beat my body and make it my slave so that after I have preached to others, I myself will not be disqualified for the prize" (1 Cor. 9:27). Nevertheless, I take comfort in Paul's words in Philippians 3:13: "Brothers, I do not consider myself yet to have taken hold of it."

There is a warning to us: we can never go higher than what God has in mind. We cannot upstage God. Whatever Plan A is for us is determined in His will. We may be disappointed. We may have other ideas, but God is not swayed.

Plan A for me is to do the work of pastor, teacher, and evangelist. Plan A for you may be to be a housewife, to be faithful to your husband, and to be a good mother. Plan A for you may be that you are to be the best schoolteacher, the best taxi driver, the best doctor, the best salesman, the best nurse.

Jesus was God. Plan A for Him was never to sin, and because He never sinned, He was exalted to the highest place. None of us will ever be exalted like Him, but we can let this mind be in us, to make the joy of the Lord our single objective. One day it will not be the end of the cycle, the end of the trial. One day it will be coronation day. We are going to see Jesus; I want to see His face, and the sight of His face will bring more joy than can ever be known at the natural level.

What joy it was for Jesus on the day He disappeared into the clouds and was welcomed home. What joy He knew; it was worth waiting for. God wants to do that for you and for me. "No eye has seen, no ear has heard, no mind has conceived what God has prepared for those who love him" (1 Cor. 2:9). God wants to give a taste of that to us, now.

Chapter 11

MAJESTY

And gave him the name that is above every name...

—Philippians 2:9

We come now to the high point of our passage where Paul brings in the name of the Lord. I never feel so unworthy in trying to expound God's Word as I do when I deal with this awesome theme, the name of the Lord. Have you any idea what it means to know the name of the Lord? Are you aware that *Yahweh*, the very name of the Lord, was not known to Abraham, or to Isaac, or to Jacob, even though he was surnamed "Israel"? God kept from His beloved patriarchs the knowledge of His actual name. There were words that described the deity, but He waited for a particular moment in time to reveal His name.

What's in a Name?

Proverbs 22:1 says, "A good name is more desirable than great riches," and in Ecclesiastes 7:1 we find the advice, "A good name is better than fine perfume."

Shakespeare said:

Who steals my purse steals trash...

'Twas mine, 'tis his, and has been slave to thousands:

But he that filches from me my good name
Robs me of that which not enriches him
And makes me poor indeed.

—*OTHELLO*, Act III, Scene III

Incidentally, Shakespeare's question "What's in a name?" would have been taken very seriously in the ancient Hebraic world, for the name was an indispensable part of the personality. It has been said, "Man is constituted of body, soul, and name." "As a man is named, so is he," so it was often claimed.

Often in the Bible we see the appropriate use of names. When Abigail sought mercy from David, she said, "May my lord pay no attention to that wicked man Nabal. He is just like his name—his name is Fool, and folly goes with him" (1 Sam. 25:25). The name *Nabal* means "fool." Abram was given a new name, *Abraham*, "the father of many nations." *Isaac* literally means "laughter," because when Sarah overhead that she was going to have a child of her own, she laughed. *Jacob* means "supplanter," or "one who takes by the heel," but God changed his name to *Israel*, which means "one who perseveres with God."

In the preceding chapters, we have been looking at our Lord's own vindication. We will continue to do so in this chapter as we examine more of the details of His exaltation that Paul includes in this section.

It is unfortunate that the definite article "the" to apply to "name" is not used in the King James Version, as I am reluctant to criticize it. But its translators clearly missed it and gave us "a name" instead. In the Greek it is the definite article that is used, and not to see that will cause you to miss the whole point. Paul said, "God has highly exalted Jesus and given to Him *the* name that is above every name."

IMITATING CHRIST

THE NAME

There are certain questions that the use of this name raises, and the first of these is, "What precisely is that name that is above every name?" Now a very strong hint toward the answer to this is found by examining the actual phrase "exalted to the highest place."

In the previous chapter we discovered from the Septuagint that in the Greek this is a word that is trying to describe exaltation above which no greater can be conceived. That is the kind of exaltation that our Lord was given. Now Paul adds that God gave to Him the name that is above every name, and we shall see there is but one possible answer to the question, "What is this name?"

Names in the Hebrew tradition, as we have already seen, are very important, not the least of which is the name of God. We learn this from Moses' earliest encounter with God.

One day Moses was at the foot of the Holy Mountain, as it was known, and he saw a bush that was on fire. He probably took no notice of it; he had probably seen bushes on fire before. But as he was watching the sheep, he kept looking at that bush, and the fire was not consuming it. Moses went to investigate, and as he came near, suddenly a voice spoke out of the bush, calling Moses by his name. It said, "Do not come any closer. Take off your sandals, for the place where you are standing is holy ground."

God informed Moses that He was the God of Abraham, of Isaac, and of Jacob, and that He had chosen Moses to deliver His people. Moses responded, "When I go to tell them that the God of their fathers has chosen me to deliver them, they are going to ask, 'What is the name of the God of our fathers?' What is your name?" Then God said to Moses, "I AM WHO I AM." (See Exodus 3:1–14.)

In Exodus 6:3, God unveiled His name for the first time; it is a name that we all are very familiar with and take for granted. It is simply the name *Lord*. It is, in fact, the English translation for the Hebrew *Yahweh*.

In the earliest Hebrew tradition, the sacred name appeared as a four-letter word known to Hebrew scholars as Tetragrammaton, four consonants, because the Hebrew language did not have vowels as we have them; they only had consonants, and we have to fill in the vowels. The four letters were YHWH. By the sixteenth century, no one knew how to pronounce it, but now scholars unanimously believe "Yahweh" is the way it is to be pronounced.

The reason for the uncertainty is that after 538 B.C. the name was withdrawn from popular usage. The rabbis refused to pronounce it. There was never a divine command not to pronounce it, but similar to other groups of people who imagine themselves to be very respectful when they try to go beyond God, these rabbis thought they were being very religious by not pronouncing His name.

This was just a superstition. God never said not to pronounce this name; in the Bible, Moses, David, and all the prophets used it. But the effect was that no one pronounced the name, and by the sixteenth century nobody knew how to pronounce it.

In 1520 a scholar by the name of Petrus Galatinus misunderstood the consonants and came up with an artificial vowel reading, "Jehovah." It is used in the King James Version a number of times. The American Standard Version of 1901 actually uses Jehovah instead of "the Lord" throughout the Old Testament.

Since then, all modern versions have laid this misunderstanding to rest by just calling the name, "Lord." In the New International

Version and the King James Version, whenever you have the capital letters for Lord in the Old Testament, remember that in the Hebrew it was *Yahweh*.

The meaning is "One who is," or "One who causes to be." "I AM" means the "One who is"; "I AM WHO I AM" is the "One who causes to be." It was the ultimate revelation of God's name, a name than which no greater name could be conceived. It was the name above all names.

Name of God

Now the Hebrew word *El* was the generic Semitic name of God or deity, and there are various combinations of *El*: There is *El Shaddai*, which means "God, the one of the mountains," and it is usually translated in the King James Version as God Almighty. There is *El Elyom*, "Exalted One"; *El Olam*, "God the Everlasting One"; *El Bethel*, "God of Bethel"; *El Roi*, "God who sees me"; and *El Eloi Israel*, "the God of Israel." Finally, there is *Elohim*, which is the most frequently used form translated "God." The very first verse of the Bible uses this plural form of the word, and it implicitly manifests a Trinitarian God.

Nevertheless, although there are all these terms, or words for God, there is only one word given in the Old Testament for God's Name: *Yahweh*, Lord. It is used 6,800 times in the Old Testament, set in capitals, LORD, or small caps, LORD. Now whenever we see the word *Lord* in the New Testament, even without capitals, it is a reference to Jesus. The Greek word is *Kyrios*, but it is the translation of *Yahweh*.

When Paul, a Jew, would use the word *Kyrios* to describe Jesus, he ascribed to Him not only deity but also the very name of *Yahweh*

Himself, for *Kyrios* was the word most frequently used in the Septuagint to translate *Yahweh*. Any Jew knew that.

Now to call Jesus *Kyrios*, Lord, was not only saying that He was God, but it was also ascribing to Him the name that is above every name. This is why Paul could say in 1 Corinthians 12:3, "No one can say, 'Jesus is Lord,' except by the Holy Spirit." That is why the confession of faith in Romans 10:9 reads, "If you confess with your mouth, 'Jesus is Lord,' and believe in your heart that God raised him from the dead, you will be saved."

WHEN WAS THE NAME GIVEN TO JESUS?

We know that this name was not given at Jesus' birth. When Jesus was born, God gave His name to Joseph through the angel: "You are to give him the name Jesus, because he will save his people from their sins" (Matt. 1:21). Does this mean that Jesus was not God at this point? Of course not! But why not give Him the name *Yahweh* then?

Just think how far Joseph and Mary would have gotten in Israel if they had announced that they had named their baby boy *Yahweh*. It would have been seen as the highest blasphemy. But there was another reason for the choice of the name *Jesus*. God initially gave His Son a name that pointed to His purpose and His work; *Jesus* means "Savior"; in Hebrew it appears as *Yoshua* or *Yeshua*, which means "the Lord is Salvation." Thus, He was always known as Jesus of Nazareth.

Let us consider, then, when the name was given. After Jesus died on the cross, He was raised from the dead, He ascended to heaven, and God the Father welcomed Him home. After thirty-three years of sinless living on Planet Earth, which included three years of ministry of teaching, healing, and preaching the kingdom of God, after the greatest sense of rejection and suffering of the worst pain imaginable, the Father welcomed Jesus into heaven. As best as we can tell, the first thing He said to Him was, "Sit down at My right hand." That in itself meant equality with God, as we considered earlier.

According to Paul something else took place at the same time. Not only was Jesus exalted to the highest place, the position that can only be described as that which belonged to God alone, but also Paul said that Jesus was given *the* name that is above every name. Had it been *a* name, we theologians would have speculated for centuries as to what it was. When Paul said it was "*the* name that is above every name," there was no room for doubt or speculation. There was only one name known in heaven and in earth and in all Holy Writ that was above every name. It was to demonstrate His *sheer majesty.*

Above Every Name

Now there have been some great names in the Bible and in history, but only one name exists that is above every name.

It is the name of the One who is worthy of our worship; it is the name of the One who fights our battles. This is what Moses told the people of Israel about their God:

> Do not be afraid. Stand firm and you will see the deliverance the LORD will bring you today. The Egyptians you see today you will never see again. The LORD will fight for you; you need only to be still.
>
> —Exodus 14:13

It is the name of the One who supplies our every need. It is the name of the One who made the sun in creation's morning and later took dust from the ground and made man after His own image. It is the name of the One who put His name in the temple and allowed His name to dwell there. It is the name of the One who has put His name in the midst of the church.

The name that is above every name is called the Everlasting One, the Most High God, the King of glory, the One who inhabits eternity, and the One who controls the destiny of nations. David asked, "Who is this King of glory?" and then answered his own question:

> Who is this King of glory?
>> The LORD strong and mighty;
>> the LORD mighty in battle.
> Lift up your heads, O you gates;
>> lift them up, you ancient doors,
>> that the King of glory may come in.
>
> —PSALM 24:8–9

Moses and the people of Israel got a glimpse of Him also, and they "saw the thunder and lightning and heard the trumpet and saw the mountain in smoke, they trembled with fear" (Exod. 20:18).

Isaiah saw the Lord "high and exalted," worshiped by the seraphim, "each with six wings: With two wings they covered their faces, with two they covered their feet, and with two they were flying. And they were calling to one another: 'Holy, holy, holy is the LORD Almighty; the whole earth is full of his glory.'" The prophet's response to such a sight was, "Woe to me!...I am ruined!" (Isa. 6:2–3, 5).

Ezekiel saw the glory of the Lord and said, "I fell facedown" (Ezek. 1:28).

Let anybody who begins to feel a bit self-righteous or moral in himself understand that name is above every name, and he will be humbled to the dust. "I am the LORD," we are told. "That is my name! I will not give my glory to another" (Isa. 42:8). God is a jealous God. I repeat; it may be a quality that you do not think is very attractive, but He is unashamedly a jealous God, and He is jealous for His name.

Paul tells us that when the Father welcomed Jesus home, the same God who said that He would not give His glory to another, He has either changed His mind or has recognized Jesus to be very God of very God when He bestowed on Jesus the name that is above every name.

It is a direct reference to the honor that Jesus deserved; it is a direct reference to the character of Jesus, as it was to the character of God. It is a direct reference to the reputation that Jesus deserved and to the worship that He deserved.

He who stooped so low now took upon Himself, from the Father, the honor above all others. He was given *the* name that was above every name. He who emptied Himself is now lifted up to the glorious ranks of equality with God and enjoyment of that dignity, which was ever His by right but to which He never clung. Now it is given to Him as His personal possession. Meekness—majesty!

WHY WAS THE NAME GIVEN?

Why, then, do you suppose that God gave the name that is above every name to Jesus? Paul answers the question:

> Therefore God exalted him to the highest place and gave him the name that is above every name, that at the name of Jesus every knee should bow, in heaven and on earth and under the earth,

and every tongue confess that Jesus Christ is Lord, to the glory of God the Father.

—Philippians 2:9–11

Paul puts it very carefully, showing that God gave the name for one reason only. He does not say that at the name of *Yahweh*, every knee should bow. It is as though a shift of some kind has taken place, a shift from the worship of *Yahweh* to the worship of Jesus. It is as though it has taken place in heaven and all creation. It is not that *Yahweh* ceases to be, but God, who originally gave the name "Jesus" to the one who was born of a virgin, now wants that name exalted, and He is called "Lord."

God has given His name to Jesus so that at the very name of Jesus every knee should bow and every tongue confess that Jesus Christ is Lord.

The Role of the Holy Spirit

This shift, having taken place, now means that Jesus *is* the name above all names. Every knee must bow to Jesus; every tongue must confess that Jesus Christ is Lord. In addition, this is not done only with the approval of God the Father, but it is also to *the glory* of God the Father. What we have here then is a categorical affirmation of the Trinitarian revelation of God.

Someone will ask, "Where is the Holy Spirit in all this?" The answer to that is found in the verse I quoted earlier, 1 Corinthians 12:3: "No one can say, 'Jesus is Lord,' except by the Holy Spirit." The reason that some people affirm what Paul says here about Jesus and some do not is because of the Holy Spirit.

The Holy Spirit confesses that Jesus is Lord. This is the very foundation of the Christian faith. By this you may know whether or not you are a Christian. If you believe this, not in your head, but in your heart, you are a Christian; if you do not, you are not. And if you do, it is not because you have done anything spectacular. As the psalmist put it in Psalm 115:1, "Not to us, O LORD, not to us but to your name be the glory." It is all because the Holy Spirit has enabled us to see the truth that Jesus is Lord.

THE THIRD COMMANDMENT

When we realize that God has not only given to us the unveiling of His name, but now has also shown us that He has given that name to Jesus, so that at the name of Jesus every knee should bow, it makes us see what God thinks of His name. That is why the third commandment is so important, "You shall not misuse the name of the LORD your God" (Exod. 20:7).

Very few people know what that means. It is a warning for fear that we abuse the use of His name, not by swearing, which, of course, is taking the name of the Lord in vain, but by being presumptuous, saying that what you are doing is in the name of the Lord.

God has given to Jesus the name that is above every name, at which name every knee should bow. That is the gospel we should preach. There is no other. Whoever you are, God says to you, "Bow down at the name of Jesus; bow down, and confess that He is Lord."

Chapter 12

LORD OF ETERNITY

That at the name of Jesus...

—Philippians 2:10

J esus' ascension into heaven was the day when Jesus was crowned. There will come a day when everybody will realize the full implications of this, but at that stage it was hidden.

In Acts 1:8 we discover that Jesus was talking to the disciples and instructing them, "You will receive power when the Holy Spirit comes on you; and you will be my witnesses in Jerusalem, and in all Judea and Samaria, and to the ends of the earth." While He was talking, they were not expecting anything to happen, when suddenly, as best as I can understand it, He just started to go up.

There was no sense of gravity. Gravity holds up on the planet, but Jesus just started to go up, and the disciples just followed Him with their eyes. The clouds took Him, or perhaps it was a mist that came down, or perhaps He disappeared right into a beautiful white cumulus cloud. All I know is they lost sight of Him.

I do not know whether He just kept on going through the universe; I think more likely that He just suddenly went into the eternal realm. We do know, however, that it was in that moment that the Father welcomed the Lord of eternity back to heaven.

In previous chapters we have considered the vindication of Jesus. In this chapter I want to look at what we might call a Trinitarian vindication. We will begin with the Day of Pentecost.

Pentecost Affirming Jesus

Ten days after Jesus' ascension to heaven, on the Day of Pentecost, the Holy Spirit descended on the one hundred twenty believers. Later that day when Peter stood up and spoke, the bottom line of his sermon was Acts 2:36: "Let all Israel be assured of this: God has made this Jesus, whom you crucified, both Lord [the name of *Yahweh*] and Christ."

Peter's sermon on the Day of Pentecost was basically in two parts: the first was an explanation of what was happening. There is a sense in which you could say that that was not a sermon. The sermon really began in verse 22. Before he preached, Peter had to explain what was going on. The one hundred twenty believers were filled with the Spirit, they were speaking in other languages, and apparently their behavior caused some to mock them and say they were drunk.

In his explanation, Peter revealed that what Joel had prophesied centuries earlier regarding the outpouring of the Spirit on all flesh was being fulfilled at that time.

Then Peter proceeded to preach and launched into the second part of his talk by saying:

Men of Israel, listen to this: Jesus of Nazareth was a man ac-credited by God to you.... This man was handed over to you by God's set purpose and foreknowledge; and you, with the help of wicked men, put him to death by nailing him to the cross. But God raised him from the dead…

—Acts 2:22–24

He brings in Old Testament psalms to show that what happened was the way it was supposed to be. That was the point of Peter's sermon. Suffice it to say that the last words of his sermon formed the punch line that I have quoted above—that Jesus was the Lord.

Living Up to Expectations

To put it another way, and to use language that Paul employed later in his epistles, Jesus apprehended what the Father apprehended of Him. Now that is a kind of a tongue twister.

Not as though I had already attained, either were already perfect: but I follow after, if that I may *apprehend* that for which also I am *apprehended* of Christ Jesus.

—Philippians 3:12, kjv, emphasis added

We see that God envisages a certain thing for us. Paul said, "I don't personally claim to have come up to what God envisages for me," which is an encouraging thing for all of us who feel that we have not done all that we could have done. When we know what God wants us to do, what He envisages for us, we all, I am sure, blush. Even Paul said, "I do not *consider* myself yet to have taken hold of it [apprehended]" (v. 13, emphasis added).

But when it came to Jesus, there was nothing that the Father envisaged for Jesus that He did not perfectly fulfill. All that the Father had planned for Jesus, Jesus did. For example, the original name that the Father gave to the Son was Jesus. As we saw earlier, the name *Jesus* means "Savior." Now that is certainly quite a name to live up to.

I do not know whether when you named your child you chose a name that means something. Most names, if you look at the etymology, have a meaning. My first name is Robert, but I do not think my father, in fact, cared what it meant. I was named after his favorite preacher, who went by my initials, RT. Sometimes we will give a name because we hope that the child will turn out like their namesake and live up to expectations.

We know that Jesus lived up to His name and came up to the Father's expectation. The name had been chosen by the Father, derided by man, feared by devils, worshiped by the angels, and addressed by the dying thief on the cross when he turned to Jesus and said, "Jesus, remember me" (Luke 23:42). He did not say "Lord." He needed a Savior, and recognizing this, he addressed Jesus by name.

Confidence in His Name

I hope that there will result from reading this book a confidence in the name of Jesus. When we grasp the power of that name, there is deliverance. We cannot underestimate the practical implication in our prayer lives of the power of the name when it is used in deliverance, healing, or whatever. This, then, is the vindication of God's Son. Now He enjoys what is rightfully His, having fulfilled all the Father's plans.

There was a time in my early ministry when no one held out any hope for me. I was a disappointment to my father; I was a disappointment to all those who knew me. They all said I had had such a promising future, but because of my theological views I had turned my back on my own inheritance. I will never forget the day I was in West Palm Beach, Florida, and in the shadow of the great First Baptist Church there, feeling so small. I felt that I was nothing.

Well, I was nothing. What do you think of a vacuum cleaner salesman who claims that he is a preacher? That is what I was in those days. I was at this church with a friend of mine, and all around me were really big-shot preachers. I just felt like I was nothing. I thought, *God, didn't You call me to preach? Didn't You give me a gift to preach?*

I felt awful. That was a time for me when God emptied me. In my case, it was not a matter of emptying myself. God just did that for me. I cannot be truthful and say that I had the humility to empty myself. He made me nothing, and it was a kindness. It meant that when I began to preach, I knew that it was God's doing, and I could not take the credit for it.

The difference with Jesus is that He voluntarily emptied Himself. He gave up what was rightfully His, and now we are told that He got it all back. He deserved to be exalted, and so He was vindicated.

Vindication of the Father

One of the most sobering and most thrilling things that I have seen yet in this section is that the Father was equally vindicated.

We mostly think of it being the vindication of Jesus, but we need to discover that there is nothing that God enjoys doing more than vindicating His children. This is because if He gets to do it, then it is His vindication. He is vindicated for what He had in mind for us. And if you want to get a hint as to how much God enjoys being vindicated, just see how it showed when He vindicated His Son.

God stresses in the Bible, "It is mine to avenge," which means that God reserves the right to do the vindicating. He does not like it when we try to help Him out, as if He needed our help.

Vengeance is His prerogative, but the problem is that, I suspect, God does not get to do it very often. I suspect it is because we do not wait for Him to vindicate us. We might say, "Well, Lord, I'll give You a couple of days. You say that You are going to vindicate me, so let's see. I'm just going to see how long You are going to take." But God does not like that. He wants us to trust Him to do it in His time and in His way.

The one time God got total vindication was because His Son totally emptied Himself and never vindicated Himself along the way. Jesus never retorted; He never retaliated. No, He just looked to the Father. In the end, the Father showed all of us how much He loves to vindicate us, because it is a vindication of Himself.

VINDICATION OF HIS WILL

God has a plan for you. He has something in mind for you far better than anything that you could come up with. We call it the will of God. You will never do better than His will. Do not ever think you can upstage the will of God. The joy you will experience because you waited on Him is incomparable, because God loves to carry out His plan, as that vindicates Him.

You may say, "Well, He didn't do a very good job with me. I have emotional scars on my life. I had this happen to me when I was a child, and I wasn't treated very nice by my parents," and so on. God says, "I know about that. Do you think that I was looking the other way? I have fashioned you." (See Psalm 139:14.)

What God wants, therefore, is to use you just as you are. God wants you to trust Him in all that has happened to you and fashioned you to make you who you are. He has an idea, and if you wait for Him, He will be vindicated, for He wants to show you what you mean to Him!

The Father's idea was that He would send His Son, the Lord of eternity, into the world, long before you and I were born, long before there was ever a church or man in the Garden of Eden. He determined it long before He created the sun, the moon, and the stars.

Take note of this: God, who had an idea about His Son and what His Son should do, also has an idea about you and what you should do. It is carefully thought out. The very hairs on your head are numbered. And God loves you as though there were no one else to love. It is the same God who sent His Son into the world to say to us, "As the Father has sent me, I am sending you" (John 20:21).

In the case of the Lord Jesus, did God make a mistake in sending His Son? Did He misfire? Was this decision right to have a people, this decision to overrule Satan's revolt and man's fall, this decision to name Him Jesus? Of course it was!

Sometimes God had to give people a new name when He had a better idea. For example, Simon became known as Peter, the Rock. But in the case of Jesus, there was no need to change the name; God had it right the first time. He called His name, Jesus. Although Jesus has now been exalted, the name is the same in heaven: "At the name of Jesus every knee should bow..." This same Jesus is made Lord and Christ. Therefore, whenever we talk about Jesus, we are dignifying the name that the Father gave to the Son. What a name!

Vindication of the Spirit

Many of us think that Jesus was able to do what He did because He was God. But that is not what the Bible says.

In Luke 4:14 we read, "Jesus returned to Galilee in the power of the Spirit." This is very interesting because it shows us that it was the *Spirit* who enabled Jesus to do all that He did. Luke 5:17 tells us the same thing: "One day as he was teaching, Pharisees and teachers of the law...were sitting there. And the power of the Lord was present for him to heal the sick." Similarly, we read in John 5:19, "The Son can do nothing by himself." It was the power of the Holy Spirit that enabled Him. This is a hint to all of us.

Our difficulty is that we want to hold on to our own gift. I have observed time and time again some very talented people not being used because they wanted the praise of men. I have noticed ministers who had a marvelous gift, but who were so afraid that it would not be recognized that their pride destroyed them. It could happen to any of us.

But with Jesus, He actually said, "The Son can do nothing by himself." That meant that the Holy Spirit vindicated Jesus. Do you want the Holy Spirit to use you? Then let the Spirit do it. It was the Spirit who vindicated Jesus all along. Paul said in 1 Timothy 3:16, "Beyond all questions, the mystery of godliness is great: He appeared in a body, was vindicated by the Spirit..."

Jesus received His joy from the Holy Spirit. This is the reason He was able to handle rejection. This is why He could cope with the way people talked about Him. He did not take it personally; He knew it was their problem, because His joy was from the Spirit. Finally, on the Day of Pentecost, when the Spirit came down, Jesus was vindicated again.

This could happen because the essential function of the work of the Spirit is to point men to Christ. Therefore, after Peter said, "God had made this Jesus…both Lord and Christ," great conviction swept over the crowd and they began to cry, "What shall we do?" (Acts 2:36–37). Three thousand were converted, all because of the Spirit's power. Filled with the Spirit, they went their way, doing everything in the name of Jesus. The name of Jesus became the dominating theme.

The Name of Jesus

One day Peter and John passed the Beautiful Gate in the temple at Jerusalem, where sat a crippled man, forty years old, who had never walked in his life. He was a beggar, and when Peter and John passed by, he put his hand out for alms. Peter stopped and said, "We don't have any money. But what we have, we give you. In the name of Jesus Christ of Nazareth, rise up and walk." And he did. (See Acts 3:1–8.) The name of Jesus was the key.

This was recognized so clearly that the disciples were threatened again and again, "Do not teach in that name." The authorities kept saying, "Did we not tell you not to speak in that name?" The authorities hated the name. Yet, when the followers were beaten, they rejoiced that they were counted worthy to suffer for the name.

It was the name that the Father had given to the Son. So if today we are filled with the Spirit, we will affirm the name, Jesus. God has promised how things are going to turn out.

> The mystery of his will…to be put into effect when the times will have reached their fulfillment—to bring all things in heaven and on earth together under one head, even Christ.
>
> —Ephesians 1:9–10

Although the future may seem uncertain, we know things will turn out because of what has already happened. God has exalted His Son and given Him the name that is above every name, that at the name of Jesus every knee should bow. So one day, everybody will bow. There is a day coming when everybody will be in total agreement that Jesus Christ is Lord.

The difference between the Christian and the non-Christian is this: the non-Christian will eventually bow the knee; the Christian does it now.

Chapter 13

LORD OF INFINITY

Every knee should bow...

—PHILIPPIANS 2:10

We learned from Philippians 2:9 that God has given to Jesus the name that is above every name. And yet Jesus let His disciples discover the authority of His own name, even before He was crucified, raised from the dead, and exalted.

He let them discover it, for example, when in the words of Matthew 10:1, "He called his twelve disciples to him and gave them authority to drive out evil spirits and to heal every disease and sickness."

It seems they were beginning to grasp it when in Mark 9:38, John said, "Teacher...we saw a man driving out demons in your name and we told him to stop because he was not one of us." They were starting to understand the power that Jesus' name engendered. In Luke 10:17 the seventy returned after their mission and excitedly announced, "Lord, even the demons submit to us in your name."

What is important about each of these occasions is that when these things took place, they did not have Jesus physically with them. This is the point: the authority of Jesus' name is exercised not by Jesus Himself, but by others.

Jesus further informed His disciples that after He was raised from the dead, "These signs will accompany those who believe: In *my name* they will drive out demons" (Mark 16:17, emphasis added). This was just prior to His departure from them. In preparation for this event, He had previously told them, "I am going to leave you, and the Holy Spirit will come." The words Jesus uses here are very interesting. He said, "...the Holy Spirit, whom the Father will send in *my name*" (John 14:26, emphasis added). Therefore, even the Father sent the Spirit in Jesus' name.

But Jesus did not Himself exercise the authority of His own name. His presence was sufficient. Only when He was not there was the authority of Jesus' name exercised by a second party.

Two Greek words are translated "power" in the King James Version. One is *exousia*, and the other is *dunamis*, from which we get the word "dynamite." It is the first of these words—*exousia*, which means "authority"—that I want to consider here.

On at least two occasions, Jesus used the word *exousia*: in Matthew 28:18, "All *authority* in heaven and on earth has been given to me," and in His High Priestly prayer in John 17, "Father...you granted [me] *authority* over all people" (vv. 1–2). For Jesus was the Lord of infinity.

Both instances are references to the authority of Jesus' own person. This authority Jesus always had while He was physically present. Of course, when He was actually there He didn't have to say, "I am doing this in My name." He just spoke it. When He finished the Sermon on the Mount, He was regarded as one who had taught them with authority, unlike the scribes (Matt. 7:29).

"Many who were demon-possessed were brought to him, and he drove out the spirits with a word" (Matt. 8:16). The centurion who sought His aid said, "Just say the word, and my servant will be healed," because he perceived in the person of Jesus this authority (vv. 8–9). When Jesus raised Lazarus from the dead, He did not say, "Lazarus, come out in My name." He did not have to say that; He was there physically. He merely said, "Lazarus, come out," and Lazarus moved and came out of the grave (John 11:43). Therefore, Jesus did not have to refer to His name when He was physically present. He *was* the Lord of infinity.

As a matter of fact, Jesus never exalted His own name; He acted in the Father's name rather than His own. He said, "I have come in my Father's name" (John 5:43). When He taught His disciples to pray, He said, "Our Father in heaven, hallowed by your name" (Matt. 6:9). He said in John 17:6, "I have revealed you [Greek, "your name"] to those whom you gave me."

The meaning of this authority is that others invoke all that Jesus would do by Himself. Thus, if I do something in Jesus' name, I do what He would do had He been there. It is as though I stand in proxy for Him. This is a most high but very solemn responsibility and privilege. It means that I can do nothing that He would not do. That may cause me to reassess my language and actions when I claim to be doing something in Jesus' name.

TRANSFERRED AUTHORITY

Paul states the authority of Jesus' position: "God exalted him to the *highest* place" (Phil. 2:9, emphasis added). He further refers to the authority of this preeminence, "At the name of Jesus every knee should bow, in heaven and on earth and under the earth."

It was therefore a transferred authority. God gave to Jesus the name that is above every name, so that at the name of Jesus, every knee should bow. We could say that there was a transfer of authority within the Godhead. There was, as it were, a reshuffling within the persons of the Trinity. The first person of the Trinity gave His name to the second person of the Trinity. The old intimate name of God, which was simply Lord, from the Hebrew *Yahweh*, was given to Jesus. This was so that every tongue should confess that Jesus Christ is Lord to the glory of God the Father.

Have you ever considered, however, what happened to the first person of the Trinity? If God gave the name that is above every name to the Son, what about the first person of the Trinity? He becomes known as the Father. Jesus never called Him anything else but the Father apart from one occasion when, on the cross, He called out, "My God, my God, why have you forsaken me?" (Matt. 27:46).

This transfer of authority really began when the second person of the Godhead became man. (When referring to numbered persons of the Trinity—first, second, third—it does not refer to any term of greatness. Rather, it is how they are revealed to us in the unveiling of the Godhead. It is just a manner of speaking.) The second person was called *Logos*, a Greek word translated "Word." "In the beginning was the Word, and the Word was with God [showing the Trinitarian relationship], and the Word was God" (John 1:1). But then we are told in John 1:14 that "the Word became flesh," so that humanity was given to the second person of the Trinity; yet Jesus retained the full authority of the Godhead.

The first transfer was from the *Logos* to humanity; the second transfer was made as the person of Jesus leaves this present earth and goes to the right hand of God to receive the title *Yahweh*, or Lord.

Before He departed to heaven, Jesus deposited His name with the church, so that we on earth have the authority of His name.

Therefore, when Jesus said, "I will go away," those who were given the Holy Spirit had authority to act in Jesus' name. It could only be done, of course, as they were walking in the Spirit, which is what Peter and John were doing in performing miracles.

When you are walking in the Spirit, you never know the opportunity that might be given you. By walking in the Spirit, you have at your fingertips the power to change everything around you. That is what Peter and John were doing when they came across the crippled man we considered in the previous chapter.

Having healed the man, it was as if at this point Peter had to call a press conference. He said to the onlookers, "Do you think that it is by our holiness, by our power that this man walked?" (There is only one explanation, His name, referring to the name of Jesus.) It is "by faith in the name of Jesus, this man whom you see and know was made strong" (Acts 3:16). It was the authority of the name of Jesus that had accomplished the miracle. But Jesus was not present. He was at the right hand of God. Yet, here they were below, walking in the Spirit, and they did exactly what Jesus would have done had He been there. By walking in the Spirit they could do these things because of a transferred authority.

TOTAL AUTHORITY

Paul also wrote, "At the name of Jesus *every* knee should bow" (emphasis added). On one occasion the apostle Paul put it like this: "In the past God overlooked such ignorance, but now he commands all people everywhere to repent" (Acts 17:30). Jesus is now the only name by which anybody can be saved (Acts 4:12). The authority of Jesus' name is total.

The offense of the Christian faith is more evident today than ever. We are doing what we do under the authority of His name. And if the world hates us, it is because they hated Him. This authority, we might say, is total in three ways.

First, no one is *exempt*. The Bible tells us that every knee shall bow. Whoever you are, you are commanded to bow the knee to Jesus.

Second, Jesus Christ in Himself has all *authority*. He says in Matthew 28:18, "All authority in heaven and on earth has been given to me." Thus, the whole of the Godhead, as it were, was invested in Jesus. All authority was given to Him who was the Lord of infinity.

Third, it is total because He commands complete, total *submission*. Every knee must bow. The great commandment of the Old Testament was, "Love the LORD your God with all your heart and with all your soul and with all your strength" (Deut. 6:5).

The total authority of Jesus, therefore, demands our complete respect and acknowledgment of His power.

TRANSCENDENT AUTHORITY

Another aspect of Jesus' authority is that it transcends space, time, and mankind. The word *transcend* means "to rise above, to surpass, to excel." Transcended authority is authority that overrules everything. What is it, then, that Jesus transcends?

Everything in heaven

Paul tells us that it is everything in heaven. This includes every creature that by the sovereign will of God happens to be in heaven. "Let all God's angels worship him" (Heb. 1:6). That means that the cherubim who dwell in the very presence of God worship Jesus, bowing before Him. The seraphim who do not rest day or night, saying, "Holy, holy, holy is the LORD Almighty," worship Him (Isa. 6:3).

It means the archangels bow to Jesus. The Word that was made flesh, who died on the cross, and who was raised from the dead and sits at the right hand of God is the object of worship by the archangel Michael, by Gabriel, and by all of God's angels.

It means that the saints who are dead, even those who died in Old Testament times, who in heaven were worshiping the Lord God at the moment the Son of God returned to heaven and the Father said, "Sit at My right hand," are now bowing the knee to Jesus.

Everything on earth

His transcendent authority also includes the earth. This means you, me, and all those whom we meet. Essential to a real response to the gospel is bowing down, as a sinner, before Jesus Christ the Lord. He is God, and the inevitable result of conversion is the worship of Jesus Christ.

It is not something that simply takes place at 11:00 in the morning and 6:30 in the evening on Sunday. Worship is a lifestyle. It is a totality of dedication of thought, word, and deed to Jesus. When you become a Christian, you bow to Jesus, meaning you submit to His rule. It means a change of management, and He sits on a throne in your heart. If you say, "I don't like that kind of Christianity," then you are not saved.

Everything under the earth

Jesus' transcendent authority also covers, as Paul says, those things that are "under the earth" (Phil. 2:10). The Greek word here, *katachthonion,* is found nowhere else in the New Testament.

In classical Greek, it was a word that referred to the infernal gods, and it is obviously a reference to fallen angels and to Satan, who are commanded to worship Jesus Christ. On one occasion Jesus met a demon-possessed person, and the demon cried, "What do you want with us, Son of God?...Have you come here to torture us before the appointed time?" (Matt. 8:29).

When Satan was cast down from heaven, as we can read in the description in Revelation 12:12, we are told that he was filled with fury, because he knew that his time was short. Satan hates the name of Jesus, because he hates God. Yet even Satan is commanded to bow to the Lord Jesus Christ.

In Jesus' name we have authority over Satan now, because Jesus Himself had authority over Satan. Incidentally, some day you and I will personally witness Satan's end:

> The devil, who deceived them, was thrown into the lake of burning sulfur, where the beast and the false prophet had been thrown. They will be tormented day and night for ever and ever.
>
> —REVELATION 20:10

When we go in the name of Jesus, we find that we have invested in us this authority over Satan.

TRANSMITTED AUTHORITY

This leads me to one aspect of the authority of Jesus' name that has been implied throughout this chapter: that is, this authority is transmitted to us. Believe it or not, it is an authority offered to all men.

We read in John 1:12, "To all who received him, to those who believed in his name, he gave the *right* to become children of God" (emphasis added). Those who accepted it were given sonship. Believing in the name of Jesus gives us the authority of sonship.

Moreover, we are told that just by calling on His name, we have assurance of eternal life: "Everyone who calls on the name of the Lord will be saved" (Acts 2:21).

An authority is transmitted to those who believe and become His representatives as they walk in the Spirit. This is what Peter and John were doing. It is a great responsibility, for the wrong person using the name of Jesus can get himself into all kinds of trouble.

Take, for example, the story in Acts 19. The sons of Sceva who had overheard other people casting demons out in the name of Jesus decided to try the same approach. They used a formula, "In the name of Jesus, whom Paul preaches, I command you to come out." But the evil spirit answered and said, "Jesus I know, and I know about Paul, but who are you?" The man in whom the evil spirit was leaped on them and overcame them. Indeed, we are told that all the men were severely beaten. (See Acts 19:13–16.) They were out of their league.

Yet if we have been given the Holy Spirit, we can act in His name. Because it is a transmitted authority, to the degree that we are filled with the Spirit, we can do what Jesus could do were He physically present.

When the day of our vindication comes, we will find that the degree to which we really have acted under the true authority of Jesus' name will be the degree to which our name is cleared. Nevertheless, on that day it will not be our name that we will be thinking about.

In heaven, therefore, the center of it all will be that One who was God and who became man, who became nothing; whose name was hated and feared, but whose name has now been cleared. Now, God commands all to bend the knee to Him.

All hail the power of Jesus' name!

IMITATING CHRIST

Chapter 14

TO THE HEIGHTS OF HIS THRONE: THE HONOR OF JESUS' NAME

...that at the name of Jesus every knee should bow, in heaven and on earth and under the earth...

—PHILIPPIANS 2:10

Philippians 2:10 is one of those verses in the Bible that is a close translation of part of Isaiah 45:23, which reads, "Before me every knee *will* bow; by me every tongue *will* swear" (emphasis added). And it is found again in Romans 14:11: "It is written: 'As surely as I live,' says the Lord, 'every knee *will* bow before me; every tongue *will* confess to God'" (emphasis added).

There is, however, a subtle difference to be found in Paul's use of these words in Philippians 2:10 as he puts the phrase in the subjunctive mood rather than the future tense. He says, "Every knee *should* bow," whereas Isaiah (and when Paul quotes him in Romans) says, "Every knee *will* bow." Why is there this difference?

I believe there is an answer, and that it is what Isaiah prophesied and what Paul referred to in Romans shows what all men will ultimately, categorically, and unconditionally do. In contrast, in Philippians 2:10, we have the assertion of God's claim over all men, and in the light of Christ's humiliation and exaltation, it is what they should do in the meantime. The passage in Philippians refers, therefore, to what Christ has earned by virtue of His humiliation and His death, resurrection, and ascension. All who see this now are called "saved." Those who do not see it, but wait until the last days when Isaiah's prophecy will be fulfilled, will be damned, even though they too confess that Jesus Christ is Lord at that time.

This simple distinction, which one word can cause in a verse, nevertheless has far-reaching implications when we consider the subject of this chapter—the honor of Jesus' name.

The Reputation of Jesus' Name

According to Paul, the reputation of Jesus' name is in three places: heaven, earth, and under earth.

In heaven

Heaven is the place where the name of Jesus has the reputation that it deserves. That is the one place where the name of Jesus is not just honored, but it is honored in the way that it deserves. Jesus' vindication was not on earth but in heaven.

Perhaps you want vindication, or maybe you have been vindicated in God's eyes, but you want others to know. Jesus was vindicated, and the ones who made Him suffer did not see it. It is only those who matter who see it, and we need to get it in the right perspective. We can enjoy the vindication that God wants to give. Vindication in heaven—that is what matters.

In heaven there is a clear understanding of what Jesus did. All He did throughout His earthly life in obedience to God, and all that He did on the cross, they understand. It is the same for us. What we may have given up, as well as what we may have suffered, is known *there* at the precise moment. Thus, the Spirit can vindicate us, too; we get our joy knowing that heaven knows.

That does not mean that we do not feel bad here below. Years ago my wife and I were in Saint Petersburg, Russia. I went there with great suspicions of those who were entertaining us. I thought my translator had to be KGB approved, and the entire time I doubted that he was a real Christian. After we had been there a while, however, I began to see that he was a man of God. He was suffering in a way that he could not tell me, and he tried to hide it. I once looked at him and said, "Sergei, you suffer, don't you?" And he just walked away saying, "No one knows; no one knows."

Yet, in heaven they know, and that is a great comfort.

On earth

On earth there are two categories of men: saved and lost. Those who are saved have a measure of understanding of the honor and of the deserved reputation of Jesus' name. But it is, at best, a vague understanding.

In the old hymn "There Is a Green Hill Far Away," there are two lines that say:

We may not know, we cannot tell,
What pains He had to bear.

These lines really grip me, for they relate directly to our perception of the honor of His name. What is meant is, the degree to which we see His glory enables us to be more unashamed of Jesus in our day-to-day living.

Indeed, the more we see this, the more unafraid we will be. Do you want to know what will emancipate you from the fear of man? It is just getting a glimpse of the honor of Jesus' name. I quote from Acts

5:41, "The apostles left the Sanhedrin, rejoicing because they had been counted worthy of suffering disgrace for the Name." When we do not appreciate His name, we show that we are ashamed of Jesus, which is why we are afraid to go out there and witness for Him.

We will develop a true indignation against the abuse of His name to the degree with which we see His glory. It will break our hearts when we see His name dishonored; we will be grieved. Similarly, rather than rejoice when a brother falls, we will be grieved because we know what it does to the Lord's name in the world.

This is relevant particularly in the church. The degree to which we, the church, which is called by His name, are given to see His glory is the degree by which we will begin to restore the honor of His name to the world. That is what we are called to do, and there is only going to be one way to do that—we must love one another. There must not be one person who is avoided, treated with suspicion, talked about, or distanced from. Instead, there must be fervent love among the brethren. When that happens, we will begin to restore the honor of His name.

It will not be because one group can then claim to be right. As long as we think like that, we are thinking of our name. We have to realize that our name does not matter. Jesus' name must take priority.

That, however, is the saved on earth. What of those who are lost? They have no understanding of His honor whatsoever. In 2 Corinthians 4:3–4, they are described by Paul in two ways: lost and blind. They are lost because "if our gospel is veiled, it is veiled to those who are perishing [lost]." And they are blind because "the god of this age has blinded the minds of the unbelievers, so that they cannot see the light of the gospel of the glory of Christ, who is the image of God."

The unconverted, therefore, do not realize what they are doing when they dishonor His name. When they become Christians, they are ashamed of their behavior, and they want to live in a way that honors God. The words of John Newton's tombstone record just such a change of heart: "John Newton, Clerk, once an infidel and libertine, a servant of slaves in Africa, was, by the rich mercy of our Lord and Saviour Jesus Christ, preserved, restored, pardoned, and appointed to preach the faith he had long labored to destroy." He never got over being saved. His famous hymn "Amazing Grace" reads:

I once was lost, but now am found,
Was blind, but now I see.

Yet, if we who are saved see the honor of His name only dimly, those who are lost do not see it at all.

Under the earth

The phrase "under the earth" refers to the infernal gods of Greek literature. We understand it to mean that Jesus is known in hell. That is the way it was put in Acts 19:15; the evil spirit said, "Jesus I know, and I know about Paul, but who are you?" What is the reputation of Jesus in hell therefore?

To begin with, it is well known that there is no remote corner of hell where the name of Jesus is unknown. The vast regions of the fallen spirits would know all about the name of Jesus. His name may not be known in the remote corners of this globe, but it is known in the regions of the damned.

What's more, His name is feared in hell. Nothing terrifies the demons like the name *Jesus*. Nothing causes Satan to panic like faith in the name of Jesus. Faith in that name turns darkness into light, guilt into freedom, shame into dignity. And when there is faith, sickness into health. That is the extent of the reputation of His name.

The Actions Required

Taking Philippians 2:10 literally, we are bound to place these words into action. This verse calls us to do three things: it calls us to assume a certain *posture*, it calls us to *profess* the name, and it calls us to affirm our *priorities*.

Posture

Paul is referring to a certain posture, specifically, that "every knee should bow." Although we may interpret this metaphorically, it is worth noting that in ancient times they did not take it metaphorically. Back then, falling down on your knees signified worship. During the time of King Nebuchadnezzar's golden image, the herald cried out:

> O peoples, nations and men of every language: As soon as you hear the sound of the horn, flute, zither, lyre, harp, pipes and all kinds of music, you *must fall down and worship* the image of gold that King Nebuchadnezzar has set up. Whoever does not fall down and worship will immediately be thrown into a blazing furnace.
> —Daniel 3:4–6, emphasis added

This was just seen as the way one should worship.

In the same book we read of the rivalry some felt with regard to Daniel. The men of the court did not like Daniel; he was head and shoulders above them, but there was no way they could get at him except through his worshiping God. "Ah!" said someone, "I think I know a way. We just come up with this decree that no one can worship anyone but the king."

How did Daniel respond? When he knew that the decree was signed, he went into his house, opened his windows toward Jerusalem, and three times a day he got down on his knees and prayed, giving thanks to his God, as he had done before (Dan. 6:10). He did not have to do this. He could have gone to another part of the room or closed the windows.

I wonder if you have ever noticed that Jesus also knelt. When He prayed in the Garden of Gethsemane, He went a little further than the others and fell on His knees. Jesus did that (Luke 22:41). Do you want your prayer life to be like that of Jesus?

In Revelation 1:17, John wrote, "When I saw him, I fell at his feet as though dead." In the Bible, when people were slain in the Spirit, they fell forward onto their faces (Ezek. 1:28). Of course, posture in any form can be superficial if our hearts are not pure, but I am haunted by this fact: that the great saints knelt. In Acts 20:36, after Paul addressed the elders of the church at Ephesus, "he knelt down with all of them and prayed." In Acts 21:5, Luke wrote, "When our time was up, we left and continued on our way. All the disciples and their wives and children accompanied us out of the city, and there on the beach we knelt to pray."

Profession

Our verses in Philippians, however, presuppose not only a certain posture, but also a certain profession or declaration. Paul says, "Every tongue [should] confess."

Why does he mention the tongue? Well, it is how you make yourself understood. Others know where you stand by what you say. The tongue is the instrument by which others know what you believe. To confess Jesus Christ to be Lord separates you from the unsaved. If you confess Jesus Christ to be Lord, it shows what has happened internally to you, because no man can say that Jesus is Lord but by the Holy Spirit.

Priority

Paul also indicates that a certain priority is assumed: "Jesus Christ is Lord to the glory of God the Father." This means that you bow to no other.

There is that famous phrase, "He must be Lord of all, or He will not be Lord at all." Therefore, you must make your own name nothing. You must put the honor of your name in suspension. Do not try to clear your name; do not try to pull strings and say, "Here's what I meant. Here's what I really said. Let's get this right." Do not try. Let them think the worst, because it is the honor of His name that is your priority. Your reward will be in heaven, and you must wait until then. That will be perhaps one of the things that will make heaven, heaven.

Jesus Christ's name and honor must become central; all you must live for is for the honor of His name. If your job compromises the honor of His name, you must let it go; it is not worth it. No matter how much money you make, let it go. Go to washing windows or mopping floors rather than let anything you do compromise the honor of His name. If your family compromises the honor of His name, then you are doing something wrong. If pleasure compromises the honor of His name, you are in sin.

Your future, your plans, your marriage, your career, your vacation, your choice of friends, your use of money—all that you do must be subservient to the honor of His name. Otherwise, though you may call Him Lord, He is not enthroned in your heart.

Why Should We Bow?

I come now to the reason every knee should bow. The answer is because He is Lord. Our verse says, "Every knee should bow…and every tongue confess *that* Jesus Christ is Lord." The Greek word is also translated *because* He is Lord.

Here is a point sometimes overlooked; He is Lord already. We do not make Him Lord, but we merely acknowledge what is true. Our conversion does not change Him; conversion changes us so that we see what is true. We must bow the knee, therefore, because Jesus Christ is Lord, both of the living and the dead (Rom. 14:9). We do not change anything by our confession. We are just coming to terms with what God has already declared.

There are two ways of honoring Jesus' name: voluntarily or involuntarily. Those who do it now show faith is at work. Those who do it on the last day will do it by sight. You may battle against conversion, and you may win the battle, but God will win the war. Some day, every knee shall bow and every tongue shall confess that Jesus Christ is Lord. So the one who is persuaded now shows God's invincible grace; the one who does it now shows that he has been saved. Those who do it later will do so because they have no choice, and they will be damned forever and ever.

Honoring God's Name

I could not finish this chapter without encouraging you to make the honor of Jesus' name the highest priority in your life. I do not make New Year's resolutions as such, but every year the first thing I write in my diary, on January 1, will be something with reference to my prayer for the coming year.

When I was preparing for this book, these were my words: "A jealousy for God's name." That has been my burden throughout, and it seems to me that for all of us to come to this would solve the problem of our jealousy. Jealousy is the sin nobody talks about, and it is most certainly the sin to which nobody admits. Yet how it crops up!

Having a jealousy for God's name, however, will change our perspective. If I revere the name of Jesus, I will prefer the honor of the one whose gift is exalted. What I will not do is say, "I have a gift that is better than his. I don't know why they don't use me." If I honor His name, I will prefer the honor of the one whose gift is needed and whom God selects. God may select someone inferior to you, but if that is the way He chooses to honor His name, then you should honor it, because He must be doing it right; He has His reasons for it.

Maybe in your opinion that person does not deserve to be exalted, and maybe that is not whom you would have selected, but if that is what God has done, to show that you honor His name, you will make that subservient. You will make your name subservient to the honor of His name.

Most denominations are started, and most churches are divided, I fear, not because of real theological integrity but because of personal rivalry. This is why the honor of Jesus' name is camouflaged in the modern church. We convince ourselves that we honor the Lord's name, but what we are really saying is, "I've got it right; therefore, exalt me." But there are a million others crying to God in the same way.

We need to look again at the third commandment, "You shall not misuse the name of the LORD your God," for this is a way of using the Lord's name to prove He is on your side. Before long you have a million people fighting each other, but all claiming the name of the Lord. But every one of them is misusing the name of the Lord.

Too often when we invoke the name of the Lord, we merely use it to justify everything we do. We say, "Well, I know I've got it right; therefore, it is the honor of the Lord that I am really after." It is not; it is our own honor. Sadly, it is true that we would prefer personal vindication to the salvation of the lost; we would rather see a fellow Christian hurt than a drunkard saved; we would prefer to have our own theological point rather than the unity of the brethren.

My fellow Christians, when we truly honor the name of Jesus, we will feel what God feels. We will hurt when He is hurt, and we will want only the honor of His name in the earth. We will say, "God, take me away; make me nothing that Your name be honored."

According to Jonathan Edwards, the only infallible proof of a gracious work is a love of His glory. I agree with him. When we have this, we will begin to restore the honor of Jesus' name in the church and in the world.

Chapter 15

CONQUERING THROUGH SACRIFICE

And every tongue confess...

—Philippians 2:11

Unity was indeed the reason why this passage was written. Throughout the study of this passage in Philippians there is one thing that have we kept in mind: that is, Paul's call to a unified church. It is something that I have touched on occasionally, but I want to look at this subject in the light of some thoughts that have arisen from this passage.

The context goes back to Philippians 1:27, when Paul said he wanted to hear that they would "stand firm in one spirit, contending as one man for the faith of the gospel." Paul understood that unity in the church is something Satan does not want, for when a church is united and the gospel is preached, Satan's interests in the world are hindered. There is nothing more threatening to Satan than a united church. Unfortunately, we could say that the devil does not have a very difficult time when it comes to causing disunity.

Do you know why? It is because the devil knows how to play into our feelings and make us feel that we are right. We all have different ideas, whether they are how the sanctuary should be decorated or how to distribute church funds. What happens is that the devil gets into the hearts of many Christians and persuades them that the Holy Spirit is guiding them.

When you are convinced that the Holy Spirit is guiding you, obviously you are going to stand for what you believe. The difficulty is that you have ten different people, each thinking that the Spirit is guiding them. That kind of problem can be a nightmare. Everybody insists that they are right while the world goes to hell. The Holy Spirit is quenched and grieved. The problem is that there are not many people whose love for God is so great that they can put themselves in perspective and be willing to lose face.

Paul knew there was only one way for the church at Philippi to be united, and that was for each one of its members to be willing to lose face. That meant sacrifice. Some do not want to do that, and they say, "Well, not me, because I'm standing for the truth. It's the honor of God that I'm standing for." Each one has convinced himself that is true.

How, then, are you going to get a church united when each one believes he or she is right? The way to do it is to appeal to the one who undoubtedly had the honor of God in mind, and that was Jesus.

Obstacles to Unity

All obstacles to unity can be summed up in four words: *pride, fear, unbelief,* and *rebellion.*

Pride is simply the refusal to say, "I was wrong," insisting instead in being able to say, "I told you so."

Fear is another obstacle because of the worry and suspicion that the wrong person will be listened to, or the wrong point of view will be accepted.

Unbelief can also be a block to the unity of the church. It shows itself in that a person is afraid that God will not step in. Therefore, he may say, "I had better handle this." This is a sign that he does not think that God is in absolute control, although it is often hidden behind the claim that God wants him to do something in His stead. Soon the person begins to play manipulator, and feels quite right in doing so, but it is unbelief.

Lastly, there is *rebellion*: sheer stubbornness to submit to the warnings of the Holy Spirit. When we hear such a warning, we say, "Well, I hope he heard that," and we refuse to apply it to ourselves. We rebel against the changes that the Holy Spirit demands.

The Problem Solved

It is no wonder, then, that Paul is almost walking on eggshells as he appeals to his beloved church at Philippi to get together. Yet he does so by appealing to them to be like Christ Jesus. We cannot escape the key words of this passage: "Let this mind be in you, which was also in Christ Jesus." If they would only be like Jesus, the problem of unity would be solved. His glory would eclipse their desire for glory.

But that is not all. Consider what Christ went through, says Paul, and how it turned out for Him. In the end, God exalted Him, cleared His name, and gave Jesus His own name, the name that is above every name, that at the name of Jesus every knee should bow and every tongue should confess that Jesus Christ is Lord, *to the glory of God the Father.* So, if everybody would just be like Jesus, who conquered through sacrifice, and be willing to lose face, says Paul, then in the end the truth will be revealed. We will be unified, and God will be glorified.

All that Paul is saying, then, in these words can be summed up as a description of true spirituality. True spirituality is becoming nothing, letting God be God, and desiring only the honor of His name.

I have been preaching now for over forty years, and I have known some great Christians. However, I think many have the tendency to begin to admire a person and begin to project upon that person far more spirituality than what is really there. I can say I have learned that the people I thought were so spiritual were perhaps not so spiritual after all. I know what it is to be disillusioned and disappointed.

The reality is, of course, that there is not a single one of us that is perfect, and if you begin to admire anybody too much, you will be disappointed. True spirituality is an exceedingly rare thing. This is a topic to which I want to return later in this chapter as we examine ourselves in the light of the glory of Christ.

There have been many sermons given and many tomes, articles, and books written on the glory of Christ. It was said of the saintly Samuel Rutherford by a longtime friend, that, "When Samuel Rutherford preached on the glory of Christ, I thought he would fly away." The truth is that if we *saw* the glory of Christ, all of us would fly away, as the old spiritual "I'll Fly Away" puts it.

Or perhaps what in fact would happen is that we would fall on our faces. As we considered in the last chapter, John recorded, "When I saw him, I fell at his feet as though dead" (Rev. 1:17). There is something "unpretentious" about the glory of Christ. Even when John fell at His feet as dead, there was nothing pretentious; John just saw what was there.

We need, of course, to say what we mean by this word *glory*. Now in Hebrew the word is *kabodh*, which literally means "heaviness" or "weightiness." It was what was striking or what was impressive. Sometimes it denoted power, sometimes splendor, sometimes brightness, sometimes praise, and sometimes worth. In the Greek it is *doxa*, from which we get the word *doxology*. In Hellenistic literature, *doxa* literally meant, "opinion," but it did not take on that meaning in the New Testament. There it basically means "honor" or "splendor" or "radiance."

But when we begin to gather all these things—the weightiness, what is impressive, splendor, radiance, opinion—we see that it is what makes a person stand out that makes others notice. We might call it uniqueness. It is what is so distinctive, but pleasant, that it leaves a person almost breathless.

The word is used in various ways in the Bible; the glory of Samson was his strength. The glory of Israel was the ark of the covenant. On one occasion when the ark of the covenant had been taken from Israel, a child was born, and they named the child Ichabod, which means "the glory has departed" (1 Sam. 4:21). In the New Testament the apostle Paul said that man is the image and glory of God. Then he went on to say that the glory of man is woman, and that the glory of woman is her hair (1 Cor. 11). Again, in Ephesians 3:13 Paul spoke of "my sufferings for you, which are your glory."

God has a glory in mind for each of His people, whoever they are. It does not mean that you will necessarily be famous, a great thinker, a great speaker, a singer, a politician, a doctor, an accountant, a theologian, or a philosopher. But God wants to make you great.

The point is that your glory is true spirituality, and it comes through tribulation: "We must go through many hardships to enter the kingdom of God" (Acts 14:22).

Although your gift under God could lead to greatness even in the eyes of men, it will never be apart from your receiving the glory that He has assigned for you. For God has a glory in mind for you, which is that you become a truly spiritual person, an unpretentious person like Jesus.

When we are pretentious, people can see it, and yet we do not have any objectivity about ourselves. We go right on trying to pretend how clever, brilliant, sophisticated, or cultured we are, but that is not spirituality. Peter said, "Humble yourselves, therefore, under God's mighty hand that he may lift you up in due time" (1 Pet. 5:6). Unless you become humble, unpretentious, and truly spiritual, all that you seek to do will not amount to a hill of beans.

When we speak of the glory of Christ, we are talking about the essence of all that He was. We could actually refer to Jesus properly as "His Glory." In fact, Paul called the very gospel that we preach "the gospel of the glory of Christ" (2 Cor. 4:4). That is what makes Jesus unique.

JESUS' UNIQUENESS

The glory of Christ was a unique glory, meaning that it could not be said of anyone else. Just before His crucifixion, Jesus looked to heaven and prayed to His Father:

> I have brought you glory on earth by completing the work you gave me to do. And now, Father, glorify me in your presence with the glory I had with you before the world began.
>
> —JOHN 17:4–5

For Jesus always was God, and therefore His glory was a unique glory—the glory of God. Yet He was man with no man even beginning to be truly like Him. He was unique, therefore, both in His deity and in His humanity. He was unique in His birth; He had no natural father. There was the uniqueness of His life—He never sinned—and the uniqueness of His death—He died as a substitute.

Paul wrote, "When we were still powerless, Christ died for the ungodly" (Rom. 5:6). He went on to write, "Very rarely will anyone die for a righteous man, though for a good man someone might possibly dare to die. But God demonstrates his own love for us in this: while we were yet sinners, Christ died for us" (vv. 7–8).

Jesus, who never sinned, has paid our debt. That is the glory of His death, and when it came to His resurrection, He is called the firstfruits of those who have fallen asleep (1 Cor. 15:20). This is the Jesus who has been exalted and now sits at the right hand of God because He is the unique, infinite God/man.

Universal and Unrivaled Glory

The marvel is that although it was a unique glory, it was also an unsought glory. Paul tells his readers in Philippians 2 that Jesus emptied Himself even though He was equal with God. And yet we want to hold on to such things that give us a feeling that we are righteous. But not with Jesus; His was an unsought glory.

My food…is to do the will of him who sent me.

—John 4:34

I have come down from heaven not to do my will but to do the will of him who sent me.

—John 6:38

One fruit of emptying ourselves is that it lessens the temptation to rival the will of the Father.

Jesus did not even offer an option to the Father. He did not argue with Him. Yet when we are so full of ourselves, we begin to take ourselves too seriously, and we think that we can do better than God's will. We begin to think we are the exceptions and put ourselves above the Word.

Jesus, though He was God, emptied Himself. How much more should we, who are finite men and women, if we are spiritual, be unpretentious? A part of the fruit of all this is that we will not seek glory. Paul could say when he wrote to the church at Thessalonica:

You know we never used flattery, nor did we put on a mask to cover up greed—God is our witness. We were not looking for praise from men, not from you or anyone else.

—1 Thessalonians 2:5–6

Having lived this life of humility and obedience, Jesus' glory is restored and enhanced in heaven. Yet God gave Him more: God gave Him universal glory, that every knee should bow and every tongue should confess that Jesus is Lord. There is coming a day in which all will be in perfect agreement, when everybody will be united.

At present we have places and people united in name only—the United Nations, the United States of America. But there is coming a day when every congressman, every United States senator, every Muslim, every Jew, every atheist, every journalist, and every television commentator are going to be in perfect agreement: every tongue *will* confess the same thing.

They are going to have to get down on their knees, all of them, because it says, "Every knee *will* bow..." (Rom. 14:11, emphasis added). All men and women will be on their knees; every tongue shall confess that Jesus Christ is Lord. It is not a question of *if* we are going to do it; it is a question of *when*. But if we sacrifice our opinions for the opinion we will all have then, it brings Christ glory now.

A day is coming when every angel will make way for the King; every human being will make way for Him, as will every demon. Then we will join the everlasting song and crown Him Lord of all. The same God who once said, "I am the LORD; that is my name! I will not give my glory to another" (Isa. 42:8), now says, "You bow to My Son and confess that He is Lord to My glory."

God calls you today to bow to Jesus and worship Him and, in so doing, give God the glory. In that day it will not be the preservation of your name or mine, but Jesus will have all the glory.

Chapter 16

BOW DOWN AND WORSHIP

That Jesus Christ is Lord...

—Philippians 2:11

The use of the name *Lord* as a title is a thoroughly British occurrence. It is applied to peers, the sons of dukes and marquesses, and the eldest sons of earls, and it is an honorary title given to certain high officials. In Britain they also have what is referred to as the House of Lords, where male members are addressed as "My Lord" or "Your Lordship." Somehow I always had an uneasy feeling about calling someone Lord. (Now that I come to think about it, I do not think I have met too many.)

However, the Greek word *kyrios*, which is translated "Lord," does not always refer to deity. For example, in the Septuagint, the Greek translation of the Hebrew Old Testament, *kyrios* is often used where it does not refer to deity. In 1 Peter 3:6, it says that Sarah referred to Abraham as "lord" (KJV). Joseph was also called lord once: "No, my lord," they answered (Gen. 42:10). Indeed, I could show many similar instances in the Old and New Testaments.

Notwithstanding, when it is used by Paul in this verse, it is to show the highest title, character, name, and honor imaginable. When Paul wanted to say the greatest thing that could be said about Jesus, he said it here: Jesus Christ is Lord. We may each have one word that we think characterizes Jesus: wonderful, majestic, or glorious. Yet the fact is that the highest, greatest, most noble, most glorious thing that can be said about Jesus is what Paul says here: That every knee should bow and every tongue should confess that *Jesus Christ is Lord.*

THE COMMAND TO CONFESS FAITH

In both Philippians 2:11 and Romans 10:9, where a similar verse appears, this declaration of Christ's Lordship is seen as a confession. Indeed, in Romans 10:9 we have the essence of what makes a person a Christian: "That if you confess with your mouth, 'Jesus is Lord,' and believe in your heart that God raised him from the dead, you will be saved."

This statement is not an attempt to build Jesus up. God would never demand that we confess what is not true. Since it is impossible for God to lie, He will never demand of us anything that is not righteous, wholesome, noble, and pure. God would never manufacture a confession that is not absolutely true, so we confess that He is Lord, because He is Lord.

We are also *commanded* to confess that Jesus Christ is Lord, and there is a reason for this. Throughout the epistle of Romans, Paul states what it is that happens to a person who believes. A great deal of the epistle is about justification by faith, grace, and the sovereignty of God. Toward the close of the epistle, however, he wants to state succinctly the end result of it all. The confession that is demanded in Romans 10:9 presupposes faith and repentance, for it embodies all that is true in the gospel and all that is necessary to have assurance of salvation.

The Tetragrammaton Enigma

In a previous chapter we considered the Hebrew word *Tetragrammaton*, by which Jews refer to the four-letter name of God. I want now to look at its translation and find out what it tells us about the one whose name it is.

An interesting aspect is that this Hebrew four-letter word has a translation in itself, and yet no one is absolutely sure how to translate it. In fact, Hebrew scholars are divided between whether to translate it "One who is" or "One who causes to be."

Either way we look at it, it makes that name above every name. If we just look at it as "the One who is," we see that the greatest thing that can be said about God is that He is. We are told that "he who comes to God must believe that He *is*, and that He is a rewarder of those who diligently seek Him" (Heb. 11:6, NKJV, emphasis added). Jesus also used these words when questioned about the fact that He claimed that His coming had gladdened the heart of Abraham: "Before Abraham was born, I am!" (John 8:58). That is when the Jews took up stones to kill Him, because they knew what He was claiming.

Yet, if we translate the Tetragrammaton as "causes to be," it is the name that gives all things their existence. *Yahweh* did not cause Himself to be; He always was and is. All that is apart from *Yahweh* owes its being and existence to *Yahweh*.

Knowledge of God's Name

When God revealed Himself to Moses, He informed Moses that he was the first man to know God by His name:

I appeared to Abraham, to Isaac, and to Jacob as God Almighty, but by my name *Yahweh* (Hebrew) I did not make myself known to them.

—Exodus 6:3

Yet we know that the name "Lord" appears as early as the second chapter of Genesis. Abraham also addressed God as Lord. So how does God's revelation of Himself to Moses set a precedent? The explanation is in the way the Hebrew word "to know" was understood.

There are two Hebrew words for "knowing" or "knowledge." One of them was "just knowing" at a comparatively superficial level, and the other was "knowing" at a most intimate level: to know all the implications. The latter word is the one that is used in Exodus 6:3, "By my name Yahweh I did not make myself *known* to them," that is, in this intimate profound way. In contrast, when God revealed Himself to Abraham, Isaac, and Jacob, it was that they saw something of His transcendence and His power within Himself, but they did not see the Lord work in such depth as He promised He would do with Moses.

What God promised to Moses was that he was going to see a demonstration of God's power, and he was to realize that the name of the Lord now was to be synonymous with what He would do. This is why Moses said to the children of Israel:

Do not be afraid. Stand firm and you will see the deliverance the Lord will bring you today.... The Lord will fight for you; you need only to be still.

—Exodus 14:13–14

When Moses lifted up his rod, Israel saw the power of the Lord in a way that they had never seen before. That is what God meant when He said to Moses, "Abraham, Isaac, and Jacob have not known Me in this way."

The point I am making is that God can reveal Himself in measure without revealing all that there is to know about Himself. That is what He did to Abraham, Isaac, and Jacob. Moreover, He could, if He chose, reveal His name to one generation and withhold it from the next. It is very interesting to read Genesis 4:26: "Seth also had a son, and he named him Enosh. At that time men began to call on the name of the LORD." Jonathan Edwards thought this might have been the first real revival in the world as he said in his great book *The History of the Work of Redemption.* It seems, therefore, that some unknown people had access to the name of the Lord, that deeper knowledge that seems to have been hidden later from Abraham, Isaac, and Jacob. It just shows that God can withhold from choice servants a fuller, deeper knowledge of Himself without leaving a deposit for the next generation to build upon. The psalmist said, "The LORD confides in those who fear him" (Ps. 25:14).

You may say, "Well, I don't know much about Tetragrammaton or Greek translations, so I'll never be anyone special." You should remember that God may reveal to you, even a babe in Christ, that profoundest knowledge. The secret of the Lord is with those who fear Him, not with great intellects or brains. Back there in the fourth chapter of Genesis, men we do not know began to call on the name of the Lord.

It causes me to pause and ask how much could be revealed in our generation to an unknown man or woman that is kept from our wider knowledge? I believe that when we get to heaven, we will discover that vast knowledge was disclosed to the simplest people who were not put in strategic positions. Once in a while God may give insights to an Athanasius or an Augustine, and the whole world is affected by it. But God can, if He wants to, reveal it to one person, with no great profile, just to show His glory.

Who Is the Greatest?

We have been looking at the name *Yahweh* in this context, but now what about *Yahweh* Himself? I refer to the Lord, God, Himself. I would have thought that common sense would cause us all to be absolutely sure that whom we are praying to, whom we are worshiping, whom we are confessing, is the one who is the Lord.

Let me ask you a question: How would you feel if after worshiping your God for so many years, you discovered that there really is one who is greater? What would you do? Maybe you would say, "Well, I wouldn't want to give up God. I have come to know Him real well." Yet surely you want to worship the Most High God. Would you keep on worshiping Him? Never.

If I were to discover that there is one greater than who I thought was the greatest, I would stop praying, and I would reassess my ways, my worship, my allegiance, and my confession. Why? Because I want to locate not only the name than which no greater can be conceived, but also the one who is greater and worship Him. I only want to worship Him who is the First and the Last.

Whenever we make the claim that we worship the Most High, the one than which there is no greater, someone is bound to ask us, "How can you be sure?" The answer to that is the Holy Spirit. No man can say that Jesus is Lord but by the Holy Spirit (1 Cor. 12:3).

It's easy to get a person to repeat a prayer, but to really believe that Jesus, who was born of a virgin, lived, died on a cross, arose from the dead, and who is the one who causes to be, cannot be done unless the Holy Spirit conveys it to you.

Indeed, not only does the Holy Spirit authenticate the truth, but He also gives an assurance by which you know you have got it right. In His strength you can face a thousand worlds and a thousand devils. This is why you can stand before men. That witness of the Spirit is given so that you know the truth beyond any doubt. This is how you know that Jesus of Nazareth is Lord, the one who causes to be, even from everlasting to everlasting.

The First and the Last

Isaiah prophesied in his book concerning God:

> "I, even I, am the LORD, and apart from me there is no savior. I have revealed and saved and proclaimed—I, and not some foreign god among you. You are my witnesses," declares the LORD, "that I am God. Yes, and from ancient days I am he. No one can deliver out of my hand. When I act, who can reverse it?"
>
> —ISAIAH 43:11–13

He went on to say, "I am the first and I am the last" (Isa. 44:6).

This is one who gave everything its existence: God, who in the beginning created the heavens and the earth. But Jesus is also disclosed as being before all things and by whom all things consist. John on the isle of Patmos records:

> I turned around to see the voice that was speaking to me. And when I turned I saw seven golden lampstands, and among the lampstands was someone "like a son of man," [whose]...eyes

were like blazing fire. His feet were like bronze glowing in a furnace, and his voice was like the sound of rushing waters....Out of his mouth came a sharp double-edged sword. His face was like the sun shining in all its brilliance.

When I saw him, I fell at his feet as though dead. Then he placed his hand on me and said: "Do not be afraid. I am the First and the Last."

—Revelation 1:12–17

This Jesus of Nazareth who died on the cross and shed His blood is the first and the last, the one whom God has highly exalted. He has given Him the name that is above every name, that every knee should bow and every tongue should confess that Jesus Christ is Lord, to the glory of God the Father. It is a command that comes from none other than God Himself.

It was Jesus Christ, therefore, who made the heavens and the earth, who came to Abraham, and who appeared to Moses in the burning bush.

The Christ

Paul wrote, "Jesus *Christ* is Lord." The name *Christ* means "anointed one." It is a name used interchangeably with Messiah, both in the biblical revelation and in the ancient rabbinic tradition.

One of the things that the rabbis and those ancients who seemed to have had the monopoly on biblical interpretation seemed to have overlooked is that "Lord" and "Christ" were one and the same person. Every tradition seems to have its monopoly, or those who claim to speak for God, who say, "You listen to us if you want to know the truth." In Israel at that time, the Sadducees, the Pharisees, the

Zealots, and the Essenes all claimed to speak for God. Yet they all missed this vital point.

It is all there, but they missed it. The same thing could happen to us. We can listen to a certain tradition, and if there are people we respect who also believe that tradition, we feel safe with it and can get so entrenched in it that we fight for it, missing such central truths. What the Holy Spirit does, however, when He indwells us, is burn off the garbage with unquenchable fire.

In his sermon on the Day of Pentecost, Peter cleared the whole thing up: "God has made this Jesus, whom you crucified, both Lord and Christ" (Acts 2:36). There is just one person, Jesus, who is both Lord and Christ.

In Israel at that time they were looking for the brilliant politician, the illustrious king, some military hero. The last thing anyone would believe was that Jesus of Nazareth who was crucified could turn out to be Lord and Christ, but Peter said that is exactly what happened! He has been exalted to God's right hand, He is God, and He is Messiah.

This tells us something about God. He is behind all this, the orchestrator of this confession. He drew up the architectural plan for Jesus to follow, and He is the One who has exalted Jesus.

We are left then with one final question, which any child reading this may ask. What happens to God, then? Has He stepped aside? Has He abdicated His deity? Has He resigned from being all that we attribute to His deity?

The answer to this is found in the last words of Philippians 2:11, "to the glory of God the Father." Just as the Lord is none other than Jesus, God is none other than the Father, the One whom Jesus addressed and to whom He told us to pray. It is obvious that not only has God not abdicated deity, power, glory, riches or sovereignty, but also that the culmination of salvation history and all that happened is right on target. It is what delights, pleases, honors, extols, and magnifies God most to confess that Jesus is Lord. It is to His *glory*, and this is the word anybody can appreciate, whatever your religion or background. Jesus Christ is Lord. Here is the way to glorify God—confess Jesus as Lord.

That is the way to honor Him, to thrill Him. There is a sense in which this is the only thing that brings God glory because there is nothing more to do. There is nothing more that the angels can do and nothing more that man can do except this, confess that Jesus Christ is Lord.

This will have an effect on you because it means that you bow down to Him. It means that you say, "I'm living under new management." It is not just a confession to acknowledge His deity, for when He is Lord, you want Him to control you. You want Him to control every secret you have. There is no area of your life where He does not have supreme honor. That is what it means to confess.

To do so is the greatest thing that can happen to man because it is what assures him that he is one of God's own: "No one can say, 'Jesus is Lord,' except by the Holy Spirit." It shows also that you have been highly favored. No greater glory can be given to *us* than to make such a confession that Jesus Christ is Lord. Neither can any greater glory be given to *God*, than to say, "Jesus Christ is Lord."

Chapter 17

THIS IS YOUR GOD

. . . to the glory of God the Father.

—Philippians 2:11

If the greatest thing that can be said about Jesus Christ is that He is Lord, as we considered in the previous chapter, then the greatest thing that can be said about God is that He is the God of glory. His glory is the sum total of all His attributes. If I had to come up with one word that describes God, it is *glory*.

I will never forget how I was introduced to this in a rather unexpected and painful way. It was the night of my ordination to the gospel ministry. Dr. N. B. Macgruder preached the ordination sermon, and he was going to ask me some questions in front of all the people. I was expecting that he would just test out my orthodoxy and make sure I believed the Bible, and one or two things like that. But to my surprise he asked me to say in one word what it was about God that was the sum total of everything that He is. I could not think of a word, and it was in front of all these people! Well, I know it now! The word that Dr. Macgruder was after was *glory*.

Anyone who seeks to know the true God eventually discovers that God is preeminently and unashamedly a God of glory. One day Moses put the boldest request that ever was to God: "Now show me your glory" (Exod. 33:18). What would make a man put a request like that? Looking at it from one point of view, it is almost a naïve, if not impertinent, request.

Can you imagine somebody going to the chief chef of Maxim's in Paris and saying, "Can I see all of your recipes?" Or it is even like Elisha saying to Elijah, "Let me inherit a double portion of your spirit."

In putting forth this request, however, Moses reflected the heart of a godly man who already knew enough about God to know that the God he met at the burning bush and at Sinai was a glorious God. Moses could see just enough of God in what he already witnessed to know that there was more that was kept from him. God was not offended by the request:

> I will cause all my goodness to pass in front of you, and I will proclaim my name, the LORD, in your presence. I will have mercy on whom I will have mercy, and I will have compassion on whom I will have compassion. But…you cannot see my face, for no one may see me and live.

> —Exodus 33:19–20

Moses had to get into a cleft in a rock where God would cover him with His hand. Only when God had passed would He remove His hand so that Moses would only see God's back, and not His face. Moses could sense that there was that in God that he had not seen, but that he knew was there.

SHEKINAH GLORY

What does Paul mean by these final words in Philippians 2:11, "…to the glory of God the Father"? I looked at this word *glory* in measure in the chapter on the glory of Jesus Christ. In relation

IMITATING CHRIST

to Jesus, we saw that the Hebrew word *kabodh,* which is the word translated "glory," originally meant a number of things. Primarily, it meant "heaviness" or "weightiness," but it also means "splendor" and "honor."

But there developed a tradition in Judaism parallel to the biblical revelation. The Hebrews would speak of the "Shekinah" glory. If you have heard of that word, you may be surprised to learn that it is not in the Bible. It is in the Targums and the rabbinic writings. It was a word devised to describe the kind of revelation received by Ezekiel:

> I looked, and I saw a windstorm coming out of the north—an immense cloud with flashing lightning and surrounded by brilliant light. The center of the fire looked like glowing metal.
> —EZEKIEL 1:4

They described these manifestations of God, the smoke filling the temple, the cloud and the fire, by the word *Shekinah.*

I have often wondered what it would be like to see it. In Ashland, Kentucky, in April 1956, there was an unusual service. I was not present, although my father was, as were many people whom I knew. A number said virtually the same thing about what happened. As the preacher was reading a portion of Acts 5, there came in the service what they called a haze, which had a yellowish-golden color, so thick that you could not see to the other side of the auditorium. It lasted maybe ten minutes. During that time power was present, and the preacher that day told me himself that for those ten minutes he had power that he never knew it was possible to have. It was almost unimaginable.

When we know what God has done from just reading the Bible, particularly in the Old Testament and in the Book of Acts, we can try to imagine the wonder of seeing a manifestation of God's own glory.

Instead, what people want today is their own glory. Each person is busy covering himself, vindicating himself, watching for his own reputation, and not wanting anybody else to be blessed unless they agree with him. The consequences tie God's hands, for He is not going to lend His name or manifest His glory wherever there are those still thinking of their own glory.

Another incident that I grew up hearing about occurred at a Methodist tent meeting in Tennessee. During those meetings great persecution took place; people were objecting to the meetings. There were stories told of people who would come to the tent, determined to tear it up, and literally take a knife, cut it, and pull the stakes so it would fall down. Instead, when they got into the very area, they were converted. The believers told how it happened. One evening those outside looking at the tent said there was literally a haze on the top of the tent covering it: *the glory of God*.

We pray to experience something of this nature that defies the natural explanation. This generation has not seen true revival. To my knowledge, the Charismatic movement has not begun to see anything like this.

People want to know why I pray for unction. They often say, "Oh, you've got it." I doubt it. Yet I know that there is a supernatural power, if we could only be trusted with it, that could descend if we wanted only the honor of God and not anything else. It may be that God would put His seal on such a ministry. This is what we long to see instead of people arguing about little things. These little things become big as people defend their corner and their opinions, while the world goes to hell. The Spirit is quenched, and nothing happens.

The Dignity of God's Will

There is another aspect of God's glory that we need to explore, not just the "Shekinah" glory or even that which Moses could not look on directly. This glory is seen as the dignity of His will. God said, "I will have mercy on whom I will have mercy" (Exod. 33:19). He is sovereign. All that God is, and does, shows not only His greatness and His power, but also His righteousness and justice.

Thus the glory of God is the dignity of His will, the rightness of what He chooses to do. For God never makes a mistake. It is not only impossible for God to lie, but it is also impossible for Him to err. The most marvelous benefit of being a child of God is summed up in Ephesians 1:8 where we read that God has "lavished on us [the riches of His grace] with all wisdom and understanding." It is wonderful just to know that we are cared for, planned for, thought of, loved, and looked after.

How precious to me are your thoughts, O God!
How vast is the sum of them!
Were I to count them,
they would outnumber the grains of sand.

—Psalm 139:17

That is how God thinks of you and me. He is no respecter of persons. Because of this care, we can never do better than God's will, and loving God's will is part of what is meant by seeing and loving His glory.

In the light of the context of Philippians 2:11, the first thing that arises is that everything redounds to God's glory. The word *redound* means "to contribute" or "to have effect," so all things contribute to His glory; they end up glorifying God. We have considered previously how all things in heaven, earth, and under the earth will bow before the Lord. Now let us consider how certain things contribute to God's glory.

Creation

The psalmist said, "The heavens declare the glory of God; the skies proclaim the work of his hands" (Ps. 19:1). In the Book of Revelation we have the account of the four living creatures and the twenty-four elders who fell down before the throne and said, "You are worthy, our Lord and God, to receive glory and honor and power, for you created all things, and by your will they were created and have their being" (Rev. 4:11). All creation acknowledges His power and glory; creation's beauty contributes to His glory.

Redemption

All things redound to God's glory, not just at the level of creation, but also at the level of redemption. When the writer of Hebrews says our Lord "took not on him the nature of angels, but he took on him the seed of Abraham" (Heb. 2:16, KJV), it shows that God looked at various options before He made a decision.

This itself will redound to His glory. Then there is God's decision to save His people by His Son's death. When Jesus died on the cross, it was not that things went wrong; it was not an accident or a tragedy. The devil thought he had done it, but God said, "I did it." As I mentioned earlier in the book, all that Christ did was to bring glory to the Father. His sacrifice on the cross and our redemption all redound to God's glory.

Salvation through faith

There is also God's decision to save men by faith. Paul wrote:

> Moses describes in this way the righteousness that is by the law: "The man who does these things will live by them." But the righteousness that is by faith says: "Do not say in your heart, 'Who will ascend into heaven?' (that is, to bring Christ down) or 'Who will descend into the deep?'" (that is to bring Christ up from the dead). But what does it say? "The word is near you; it is in your mouth and in your heart," that is, the word of faith we are proclaiming.
>
> —Romans 10:5–8

Our salvation comes by God's grace through faith, not works, lest any man should glory in his salvation (Eph. 2:8–9). We are saved by faith so that our salvation may bring glory to God.

Salvation through the Spirit

When we talk about the glory of God in redemption, we also mean God's decision to save men by the effectual calling of His Spirit.

> But we ought always to thank God for you, brothers loved by the Lord, because from the beginning God chose you to be saved through the sanctifying work of the Spirit and through belief in the truth.
>
> —2 Thessalonians 2:13

His Spirit convicts us of our fallen nature and causes us to look to Him for our salvation. What God has done is to ensure that we have nothing to do with our salvation. God has taken the whole thing out of our hands. He is sovereign. This is the dignity of His will.

How does this affect you? Your reaction to this truly reveals your reaction to seeing His glory.

Eternal Glorification

There is another truth taught in this phrase: God is capable of being glorified from without. That means that what we do can make a difference to Him. You may wonder how this claim and the prior one of God's utter sovereignty can be reconciled.

Sadly, it is a very rare situation when you can bring in the sovereignty of God and man's responsibility so completely and totally that you believe both equally. What has happened in the history of the Christian church is that people have fixed their eyes on one side of it and developed a school of thought. You have the Calvinists and you have the Arminians, and each of them will show you their scriptures to support their position. Yet they get more excited about defending their own view than anything else, and God blesses neither side.

We must understand that the same God, who works all things after the counsel of His will, has revealed Himself as one who is capable of being glorified from without: "Every knee should bow...every tongue confess that Jesus Christ is Lord, to the glory of God the Father." He is capable, therefore, of being glorified by what we do.

By our worship

When we confess that His Son is Lord by worshiping Him, this glorifies God. Prostrating before Him in adoration is an aspect of worship that is just as important to God. Otherwise, why would He bother to say that every knee should bow unless this matters?

Earlier we mentioned how there is the danger that this action can become a pattern; there are those who kneel or who lift up their arms, and they can think themselves very pious. But just a minute; the Bible encourages us to do both!

> I want men everywhere to lift up holy hands in prayer.
> —1 TIMOTHY 2:8

> Ezra praised the LORD, the great God; and all the people lifted their hands and responded, "Amen! Amen!" Then they bowed down and worshiped the LORD with their faces to the ground.
> —NEHEMIAH 8:6

Some of us can become so self-righteous and offended by a particular style of worship. Some become offended at the sight of people lifting their hands in worship. I was at a meeting where there was a charismatic gathering. They had asked me to preach, and I think about 95 percent of the people had their hands up in the air. I thought, *What a beautiful sight! It can only glorify God.*

By the angels

God is capable also of being glorified from without by the angels in heaven. We read that the seraphim, each with their six wings, two with which to cover their faces, two with which to cover their feet, and two with which to fly, worshiped Him. The thing that has amazed me about this is that they did not even say it directly to

God. We are told that, "*They were calling to one another*: 'Holy, holy, holy is the LORD Almighty; the whole earth is full of his glory'" (Isa. 6:3, emphasis added). This, then, is what heaven is all about—worship of the God of glory.

By the saints

Not only do the angels bow and worship, but so do the saints who have departed for heaven. "How do you know this?" you may ask. The writer of Hebrews wrote about the "spirits of righteous men made perfect" (Heb. 12:23). What are they doing in heaven? They are worshiping Jesus.

If you find this offensive, then you reveal things about your spiritual state that is unhealthy. The president of the college that I attended in Nashville many years ago used to say that people who are not ready for heaven would be miserable in heaven. In fact, it would be hell for them to be in heaven. Now this can be taken too far, but his point was that there are those who do not want to worship here below. They hate the thought and are repelled by it. To be put in heaven, then, would be unbearable for them. It would drive them crazy. It is a sign, therefore, of whether you have been converted if you are enamoured with the glory of God; the proof that you have been saved is that you adore such a God.

If you were an architect and could design the kind of God you would want, all you could produce would be your own projection. The German philosopher Feuerbach said that all that God is, is man's projection upon the backdrop of the universe. Wrong!

That is perhaps what man wants, but man would never have conceived the God of the Bible. It is not in man to know that such a being could exist. The God who is there, the God who is and who was and who is to come, is a God of glory. This is the way He is, and

IMITATING CHRIST

those who *know* Him, were they given the opportunity of coming up with the sort of God that they would like, would change nothing whatsoever about Him. We love Him and worship Him for being just as He is.

By Satan's folly

Even Satan is in subservience to God's decree; he is one of the beings "under the earth." This is why the devil always overreaches himself. Any time we get bitter, any time we begin to take ourselves seriously, remember that in that moment the devil has gotten in. You know then that you will overplay your hand because the devil cannot do it any other way. Yet we have authority over Satan because things under the earth are subservient to God's honor and glory. "The one who is in you is greater than the one who is in the world" (1 John 4:4).

DO ALL THINGS TO HIS GLORY

If, therefore, what we do can make a difference, it follows that the greatest thing we can do is to discover what glorifies God and then do it. Paul wrote in 1 Corinthians 10:31, "Whether you eat or drink or whatever you do, do it all for the glory of God." This is much more far-reaching, but it is possible because whatever is consistent with the Lordship of Jesus Christ will be to the glory of God.

An example of this is *praise*.

Sing to the LORD a new song;
    sing to the LORD, all the earth.
Sing to the LORD, praise his name;
    proclaim his salvation day after day.

—PSALM 96:1–2

You might say, "I don't feel like doing that right now." Do it anyway! That is what might help you snap out of it.

Declare his glory among the nations,
> his marvelous deeds among the peoples.

For great is the LORD and most worthy of praise;
> he is to be feared above all gods....

Ascribe to the LORD, O families of nations,
> ascribe to the LORD glory and strength.

—PSALM 96:3–4, 7

What a dignity is given to us that we, finite though we are, can praise Him and glorify Him!

Whatever is consistent with the Lordship of Christ means *keeping our Lord's commands.* Jesus said, "If you love me, you will obey what I command" (John 14:15). This involves saying we're sorry, forgiving another, losing face not because of the pragmatic outcome, but for the honor of God's name. This is simply a means of letting God be Himself. Then His ungrieved Spirit will work mightily; His unquenched presence will be seen and felt. God alone will be preeminent, and we will lose sight of ourselves. That is the sort of focus and dependence on God that honors Him.

"CALL ME YOUR FATHER"

If we are serious about glorifying God, because it makes a difference, we can also glorify Him by perceiving Him as Father. The words that Paul uses point to this: "to the glory of God the *Father.*"

Jesus called God "the Father." This is because they were of the same essence: there was therefore no alienation between Father and

Son. However, He also told us to call Him Father. How can this be?

We can call God Father because Jesus' blood atoned for our sins. The blood that Jesus shed on the cross satisfied God's justice, and the consequence is that, because we are joint heirs with Christ, we too can call Him Father.

Let me remind you of the most dazzling thought in the world: God loves you as much as He loves Jesus. Indeed, Jesus actually said it: "[You] have loved them even as you have loved me" (John 17:23). Now, I do not have the vocabulary to convey how much God loves His Son. I only know that God spoke from heaven again and again saying, "This is my Son whom I love; with him I am well pleased."

As a parent, I want my son and my daughter to know that they need never doubt my total and absolute love. Yet just as human parents want their children to know that they love them, so the Father in heaven wants you to know how much He loves you.

That is the kind of God we have. He does not tell us to stand in the cleft of a rock as He passes by; He just says, "Call Me your Father." By the merit of the blood of Jesus, all who love Him come before the God of the *Shekinah* glory, the God and Father of our Lord Jesus Christ, the Father of glory, and He says, "This is what I am. Love Me for being what I am because I love you as you are."

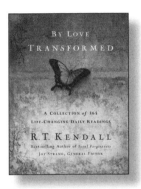
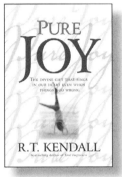
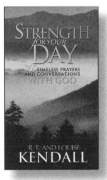